HOW TO SURVIVE YOUR CHILD'S COLLEGE EDUCATION

This book is dedicated to my parents, Rev. Edward R. Baack and Martha Jean (Lautenschlager) Baack. (Mom goes by "Jean," in case you run into her at the mall.) Mom and Dad barely survived my college experience, but still managed to provide support, encouragement, and love. I will always love them and remain thankful for their presence in my life.

CONTENTS

ACKNOWLEDGMENTS

In chapter 3, Sharon G. Johnson's work is cited. The ideas discussed in that chapter were presented in his article, "College Business Education: Some Irreverent Images, With Not So Irreverent Consequences," which may be found in the 1983 Southwest Academy of Management meeting *Proceedings* (pages 69–72), from the convention held in Houston, Texas. Several friends from the Southwest Academy of Management encouraged me to pursue publication of this book, including Peter Poole, Terry Walsh, Jan Tiefel, Rose Knotts, and Micki Kacmar.

Much of the inspiration for chapter 10, concerning finances, was derived from interactions with the accounting and billing-cashier's department at Truman State University in Kirksville, Missouri. Their work speaks for itself.

Several other thank-yous are in order. They include gratitude to Carol Publishing Group editor Lisa Kaufman, who was willing to take a chance on a professor hidden in southeast Kansas.

Christine Fogliasso, from Pittsburg State University, has been a friend and supporter for many years. Her enthusiasm contributed greatly to my efforts. Henry Crouch and Terry Mendenhall from Pittsburg State University helped to free up some time for me to work on this project.

A life in academia has meant close associations with several great teachers, including Gil Ragan, Richard Jorgenson, Rev. Clifford Hanson, Bob Trewatha, Jerry Rogers, Fred Luthans, and John Cullen.

Jon Johnson gave me several ideas and tidbits that show up in the following pages. Irene Freitas has been another terrific friend who encouraged me to write. I should also mention Meg Berrian, Julie

Vestal, and Jae Whaley from the Choral Company (a singing group I belong to), mainly because I know they love to see their names in print, and each year they vote on whether or not I get to stay in the group.

My lifelong friends John Mulvaney, Tom Prasch, and Kraig Anderson deserve my gratitude for remaining good buddies and for showing great interest in my pursuit of writing for fun and profit.

I would also like to thank my family, including my sisters, Marie (Krause) and Sharon (Baack), and my brother, Steve (Kepford). My own kids are Jessica, Dan, and Dave. Dan has become a source of material, based on his ongoing college exploits. I want to recognize my in-laws, believe it or not, for the companionship and friendship they have rendered. These would include my late father-in-law, Charles Burns; his wife, Pauline; my brothers-in-law, Landis Burns and Drew (Charlie) Burns; and my sister-in-law, Bonnie Skiba.

My wife Pam, is a great student, paralegal, friend, and proof-reader, plus she has several other skills not up for discussion here. She gives me the kind of unconditional love most husbands only can hope for, which makes her the most wonderful partner in life any man could have.

HOW TO SURVIVE
YOUR CHILD'S
COLLEGE EDUCATION

1

Getting Started

One storm passes. Another gathers. The passing storm is high school, complete with pimples and curfew violations, prom and homecoming, teenage angst, moping, confrontation, and outright rebellion. You were the one, remember, who began to despair: Will he ever grow out of it? Will she ever become "normal"? How can one person eat so much? Are this teenager and all these trivial problems ever going to leave?

Those days, friends, will soon seem like a small molehill, dwarfed by a daunting new mountain called college. No longer will your teenager's biggest challenge be figuring out how to sneak out of high school for that afternoon trip to Taco Bell. As a matter of fact, sneaking out in general becomes passé. Taking its place will be *freedom,* followed almost immediately by *consequences.* Soon enough you, the *parent,* will receive the inevitable phone call from your kid, who is trying to explain how someone with a 25 ACT (American College Testing) score could be flunking freshman English. That's right, English, the language we all speak!

College is the brave new world designed to dethrone overbearing, know-it-all high school seniors and turn them into cowering young college freshmen. It opens new doors as others slam shut. Meanwhile, you, the parent, stand there, wishing to intervene, wanting to help, and knowing you can't...or shouldn't. In high school, young people struggled for the independence necessary to establish an identity. College teaches them that they haven't finished yet. Some will succeed at this new venture. Others will fail. A few will prolong the outcome for years, taking the professional-student route.

As a parent, you are stuck somewhere between hoping for the best and becoming a meddlesome pain. If you keep your distance and let them handle college on their own, they wonder why you've abandoned them. If you get too involved, they tell you you're embarrassing and smothering them. Clearly, this is a no-win scenario. The most you can hope for is to *survive*. Hence this book. Think of it as an owner's manual, designed to help guide you through the trouble spots with a minimal amount of muss and fuss. Don't even think about winning. Instead, plot to get through this time without losing your mind, your soul, or your retirement fund.

Your child's transformation into a college student actually begins in the junior year of high school, when choosing a school begins to occupy 1 to 1.5 percent of his or her thoughts, leaving the other 90-plus percent for more important things like sex, food, and the greater social order. You can help, but you must be prepared.

Table 1.1 is a quick compilation of the things you'll need to help your son or daughter get a college education. Study it carefully. College exacts a price, from you and from your child. Make sure you know what the tab will be up front and then read on.

Choosing a College: Your Options

Selecting an academic institution is similar to dating. False starts, mismatches, unrealistic expectations, and just plain being stood up are all part of the process. There are maddening delays, and the odds are great that the schools you prefer won't be the same ones your child likes. Conflict, negotiation, and political maneuvering are to be expected. It's a nasty business.

Keep in mind that, at first, your son or daughter probably won't have a clue about selecting a college. Young people may know a few basics, such as where the good parties are, which school has the best football team, and which locations are most attractive. A high school guidance counselor may also be of some assistance. Still, it's going to

---

TABLE 1.1

An Early Checklist of Collegiate Supplies for Parents

- About $50,000, give or take $50,000
- Patience
- One car: used
- Car insurance
- Liability insurance (all kinds)
- School supplies (see chapter 2)
- 25 days off from work for:
  - campus recruiting visits
  - moving them in
  - moving them out
  - Parents day
  - graduation
  - general worry and crisis days
- 100 hours of lost sleep (per semester) to make up for:
  - late-night calls
  - insomnia due to anger over finding out their grades
  - being awakened when they're back home on vacation and they stay out all hours
  - angst over finances, especially when they call and say they need $200 more for books, *tomorrow*!
  - general worry and crisis nights
- Enough coffee to get you moving following nights of lost sleep
- Aspirin (lots)
- Tranquilizers (even more)
- Antidepressants
- Psychotherapy (eventually)

---

be up to you to help your child make a more-or-less-rational decision. It's a good idea to refresh your own memory first. Here are your basic options, along with some of their basic pros and cons:

Junior College. (These are also affectionately known as *jucos.*) There are numerous junior colleges located throughout the United States. Many Dads (as well as many major-college football and basketball coaches) think of jucos as places where academically underqualified athletes tune up for careers at a higher level. They are indeed that. However, they also can do other things. Jucos might help when:

- dollars are tight, but you want your youngster to get some early credits and exposure to college life
- your son or daughter has a few academic problems and needs remedial help
- you want to keep your offspring at home and there is a juco nearby
- your teenager is resistant to going to college at all, but agrees to take a couple of classes as a compromise

Junior-college classes tend to be less expensive and less rigorous than those offered by four-year institutions. Remember, however, the best-case outcome from a junior college is a two-year degree known as an *associate's degree*. In some instances, in fields such as bookkeeping, automobile repair, refrigeration, legal secretary, and technically oriented disciplines, this is an acceptable credential. According to a recent advertising insert in the *New York Times* (February 26, 1997), jucos prepare students for jobs in eight of the ten "hottest" occupations-of-the-future categories. Close alliances with businesses mean community colleges often can offer programs with low or no tuition (because the bill is paid by the company), with a quick transition into the labor market following graduation.

On the other hand, if your aspiring young collegian wants a four-year *bachelor's degree,* relocation to a new school will be necessary after the juco graduation. Many four-year schools won't transfer in students from a juco or accept for credit the courses taken there; this means your son or daughter may have to repeat some entry-level classes, such as science or math. Be careful to make sure you can line up a four-year school that allows most or all of the juco hours taken to be counted toward the hours needed for a bachelor's degree. Otherwise you may spend money unnecessarily on certain classes, and your kid will be bored by taking the same courses twice.

A Small Four-Year Private College. Many of these privately funded schools (not sponsored by a state or city government, though federal grants and loans normally are available) are located throughout the United States. A great number of them are affiliated with a religious group or denomination. In some cases this arrangement is mostly historical, with very little financing or direction provided by the church. In others, chapel attendance is part of everyday life, with courses in religion required for graduation. Smaller four-year schools are best when:

- your philosophy matches theirs
- your son or daughter wants or needs a great deal of individualized attention in order to succeed
- the student can gain access to scholarships, e.g., athletic or academic, that make the school more affordable
- you want your youngster to be able to take advantage of the smaller classes, greater intimacy, and other benefits of closer working relationships with faculty members
- you have a Renaissance Man–type kid who wants to do a little of everything (campus plays, choir, sports, the school newspaper or yearbook staff, clubs, etc.)

Student populations of five hundred to five thousand are the norm for small colleges. Everyone knows almost everyone else. Students often take a series of courses from the same professor, especially in their majors. Mentoring processes (one-on-one coaching as well as personal and academic counseling) are prevalent. On the other hand, if a student gets on the bad side of a key prof, watch out!

Medium-sized School: Private. Private, medium-sized schools are quite similar to smaller private and religious schools. Probably the main difference is in the variety of programs offered. In many cases these institutions choose to invest resources in specific academic programs (the University of Tulsa, for example, has worked to develop its excellent law school) and less attention is focused on other areas. Medium-sized private schools tend to be expensive. They work best when:

- you're rich
- your son or daughter can obtain scholarships or grants to soften the financial blow
- you have (or your child has) in mind a specific degree program and major that matches a specialty of the school

Medium-sized School: Public. The great bulk of the student population in the United States attends public, medium-sized colleges and universities. (By the way, the main difference between a college and a university is that universities offer graduate programs and have more distinct "schools" or "colleges" within them, such as a school of business or college of fine arts.) Often these medium-sized schools have regional names, like the University of Central Florida, or Northeast Louisiana State University, or college names such as Missouri Southern State College. Some of them have "at" names such as the University of Texas *at* San Antonio, or the University of California *at* San Bernardino. Medium-size public schools offer a variety of majors and programs, classes of reasonable size (especially at the junior and senior levels), and lower tuition costs. They are best for:

- stay-at-home students who want minimal on-campus involvement
- work-your-way-through-college students
- financially strapped students
- students who have a specific school in mind because of its location (hometown, favorite city)
- students who want to attend the university where most of their friends will be

Many regional universities have one or two specialties that make them unique. Taking a little time to find out what each school offers is the key.

Major University: Private. Among these schools are Notre Dame, Boston College, Creighton, Marquette, Xavier, and many others. Many *legacies* (students whose parents attended the same institution) attend major private universities. These schools are expensive, but usually excellent. Students who choose them may:

- be like Rudy at Notre Dame (the real "Rudy" turned into a motivational speaker in later life, so you should definitely be forewarned)
- have a Mom or Dad who went there
- think they're saints-in-training
- be geniuses who are awarded academic scholarships
- include athletes who can handle the academics and get the money via scholarships
- be locals with access to funding

Don't imagine for a second that a large church-based university is the same thing as a monastery. Strip away the trappings of the church, and one dorm room or frat house is hard to distinguish from any other. The main contrast is better access to penitence-and-forgiveness outlets.

There are also the real big league private schools like Harvard, Cornell, Yale, Stanford, Yeshiva University, and others. A fortunate group of high school seniors is both academically and financially qualified to attend these institutions. If your son or daughter ranks with them, consider yourself blessed—and poorer. Tuition at these schools ranges from $20,000 to $40,000 per year! Rich folks and geniuses (and rich geniuses) go to Ivy League and Seven Sisters schools.

Major University: Public.   Land-grant schools, such as the University of Kansas, and other state-supported universities have grown to monstrous proportions. Some, including the University of Michigan, may instruct as many as 60,000 students in any given year. It takes a unique personality to thrive in this type of environment. Many survive, but only a few end up as well-known, high-profile seniors. This is not to say that a young adult who attends a major university is getting a low-quality education. However, obtaining a good education at such campuses requires applying a great deal of individual initiative. Getting individual attention from faculty members is harder at large public universities.

Most major universities require their professors to initiate research and to publish their work in order to succeed (no to mention, to keep their jobs). Hence the phrase "publish or perish." Student employees, graduate assistants, and others close to a faculty member often receive a high-quality education. Underclassmen are usually instructed by Ph.D. candidates rather than by actual professors. There is a trade-off involved: a student gets excellent facilities and a diploma from a prestigious university, but also faces the challenge of having to develop personal training relationships and create other opportunities for individually generated learning on his or her own. Students who do well at major universities usually are:

- self-sufficient
- members of fraternities or sororities
- involved in campus activities that make them feel socially secure and included
- so smart they would succeed anywhere
- lucky, because they make friends with the kinds of students who help them get through

It is also quite possible to "hide" throughout a career at a major university, and still finish with the desired degree. Many stay-at-home students and work-your-way-through-college types are found in major public universities, because these schools charge relatively low tuition and offer flexible class schedules. Married and part-time students also can fare well in this kind of environment. Nontraditional (older) students often gain the most from a major university, as they normally are eager to learn, tend to be more certain about what they want to study, and are not intimidated by the scale of the place. Of course, "non-trads" experience similar advantages in schools of practically any size.

Your son or daughter should carefully consider all options when choosing a campus. One strategy is to start at a smaller college (possibly a juco), and finish at a larger university.

There are some often-overlooked ingredients in this critical choice that should be considered. For example:

The Pomposity Level. Pompous faculties are not limited to major research universities. Here's a simple test. Ask a professor at the school you are considering if he or she believes the school is the center of the universe. If the answer is yes (or even maybe), you have a major pomposity factor to deal with. Remember, pompous teachers develop pompous students, who go home for Christmas and look down their noses at parents, siblings, and friends.

The Hug 'Em and Love 'Em Factor. Smaller schools typically have a lot to offer in terms of faculty interaction and familiarity with students. Even some larger universities have begun to recognize the need to be warm and fuzzy. Others simply give each kid a number and let the students figure things out on their own, which is, after all, another form of education.

The Lost-in-the-Crowd Factor. Norm, a character in the television comedy *Cheers,* loved being lost in the crowd. Don't be disappointed if your child feels the same way. Not everyone wants to be class president or the captain of the team. "Getting lost and getting by" is a strategy employed by large numbers of college students, even in small places.

The Degree of Clothing. Schools in the South score low on this component. It's harder to concentrate when the girl in front of you has on nothing but gym shorts and a halter top, or the guy next to your is wearing a muscle shirt. It's not surprising that many prestigious schools are located in the cold Northeast, where it's a little easier to pay attention! Don't be shocked if your child reasons that the University of Florida seems better, and won't tell you why.

The Party-School Factor. Count the empties on the sidewalk on any given day. Enough said.

The Local Community. If the school is surrounded by barbed wire and lots of fences, this may be a message concerning what might happen when your child goes into town for a night out. A substantial amount of in-town graffiti claiming that the school sucks is another meaningful local indicator.

The Amount of Ridicule You'll Receive As an Alumnus/Alumna Based on the School's Name. Places like Slippery Rock, Ball State, William and Mary, Otterbein, Kevka, and the Philadelphia Textile School don't fare well on this factor. Neither does a college like Dana, which is usually introduced with the phrase, "Rhymes with banana." Prestige points are quickly lost in circumstances such as these.

The Number of "Huh? Where?" Comments You'll Receive As an Alumnus/Alumna. Any school named Wesleyan or Loyola has this problem, as do all of the more anonymous smaller colleges.

The Amount of Grief You'll Receive Based on a Silly Mascot or a Politically Incorrect or Weird School Nickname. Herbie the Husker was so embarrassing to the University of Nebraska administration that he was fired, until public outcries for silliness won the day. Still, alumni who call themselves the Santa Cruz "Banana Slugs," or the Purdue "Boilermakers" continue to endure lots of mascot-based kidding—and what, for heaven's sake, is a "Crimson Tide" (Alabama) or a "Cardinal" (the color, not the bird; Stanford)? The University of Oregon "Ducks" don't even have the good sense to be the *Mighty* Ducks. Of course, in the old days it might have been worse, such as when the "Bugeaters" (former name for the University of Nebraska teams) reigned on the plains. Recently, politically incorrect nicknames have created some problems for individual schools, especially when Native Americans are used as mascots. You've never seen a team called the University of Wisconsin "Rich White Guys"—now, have you? Not much to rally around there.

The Proximity of Tattoo Parlors. Concerned parents don't need an explanation of this factor, either.

Putting these factors to numbers may be helpful. Table 1.2 is a quick quiz that may help both parents and prospective students narrow their choices regarding schools of interest.

TABLE 1.2
Important, Often-Overlooked Factors in School Selection

Rate the prospective college or university using the following scale:

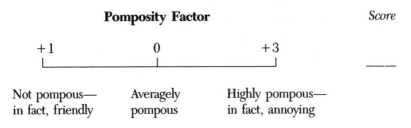

Pomposity Factor			*Score*
+1	0	+3	____
Not pompous— in fact, friendly	Averagely pompous	Highly pompous— in fact, annoying	

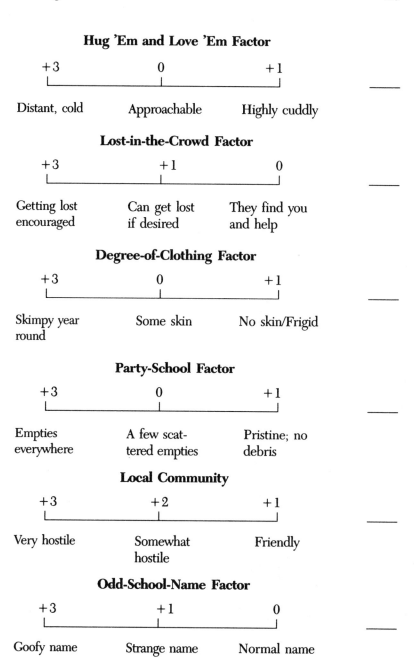

Hug 'Em and Love 'Em Factor

+3   0   +1

Distant, cold   Approachable   Highly cuddly

Lost-in-the-Crowd Factor

+3   +1   0

Getting lost   Can get lost   They find you
encouraged   if desired   and help

Degree-of-Clothing Factor

+3   0   +1

Skimpy year   Some skin   No skin/Frigid
round

Party-School Factor

+3   0   +1

Empties   A few scat-   Pristine; no
everywhere   tered empties debris

Local Community

+3   +2   +1

Very hostile   Somewhat   Friendly
                hostile

Odd-School-Name Factor

+3   +1   0

Goofy name   Strange name   Normal name

Unknown-School-Name Factor

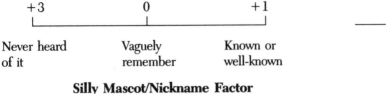

+3	0	+1
Never heard of it	Vaguely remember	Known or well-known

Silly Mascot/Nickname Factor

+3	0	+1
Embarrassing	Draws chuckles	OK Mascot

Tattoo-Parlor Location

+3	+2	0
Next door	In town	More than 5 miles away

Scoring:

Just as in golf, the higher the score, the worse the situation. Low score wins!

0 – 10	Great choice
11 – 20	Acceptable place
21 – 30	Better take a long, hard look

Explanation of Scoring

Pomposity Too pompous is bad, but so is not pompous. The faculty should have at least a little ego.

Hug 'Em As with any kind of attention, too little is a big problem, but too much isn't the best, either. Kids do need to grow up.

Lost in the Crowd Every student needs some attention, and the school should have a process to find individual students, if need be.

Degree of clothing Too skimpy, too distracted—but too bundled up isn't ideal either. The students are young; they need to release *some* hormones. A cute babe or hot hunk may be the primary motive for attending a class he or she might otherwise skip!

Party School Too many empties, too many derelicts. Still, it may be too much to expect that students will never imbibe. Kids will argue that they need to relax sometime.

Local Community If the college hasn't made at least a few locals mad, the faculty must be made up of all Casper Milquetoast types. Students need controversy, stimulation, and challenging ideas to grow.

Odd School Name In this case, normal may be better or best.

Unknown School Who wants to be from a college no one has heard of?

Silly Mascot/Nickname The key here is balance. A mascot should draw a few smiles, not derision. Also, it seems safer to have a noncontroversial nickname.

Tattoo Parlor The farther away it is from popular watering holes for students, the better.

Junk Mail: The Adventure Begins

At first it will seem innocuous enough—a few phone calls, along with some form letters and maybe a postcard or two. Soon the trickle escalates into a deluge. Mail-based recruiting will be overwhelming for those with scholarly advantages or athletic ability. Every high-school senior receives some mail, and the sorting process can become an annoyance.

Your graduating high school senior is also likely to be bombarded with brochures, cards, letters, and calls promoting credit cards, and others extolling the opportunity to be all he or she can be, in one military form or another. Since the kid is out with friends all the time, guess who gets to answer the phone and sift through the mail? There is an outside chance you'll be pleased to deal with some of it, since it does at least signal the possibility that your teenager will be moving out soon!

An emerging new form of solicitation and access to information about individual universities may interest you and your high school senior. It's the World Wide Web. Nearly every college with any amount of technological pretentiousness now has one or a series of website home pages. These allow interested parties to call them up on the Internet and "tour" the campus without ever leaving home! Many forms of basic information may be found at these http:// www@campus. aren't-we-cool.com addresses. If your family is computer oriented, you've probably already taken advantage of these offerings. Those who are just moving onto the information super-highway might consider getting the local public library staff or a computer store employee to help them surf the Net of college opportunities.

Before you go any further, some major decisions must be made. There are two main items to consider. The first is about money. The second is about everything else. Finances create decision rules. For some parents, it is necessary to squeeze out every possible dollar in order to make it possible for a cherished child to attend college. For others, money is no object and a whole different set of selection criteria is used. Everyone wants what is best for their kids. The following chapters are designed to help you untangle the web of deception and bureaucracy created by college administrators, so you finally can orchestrate the eventual marraige of your youngster to his or her school. At best parents are matchmakers. At worst...well, maybe it's not wise to get into what's worst—at least not yet. After all, you're just getting started.

2

Finding Funding Is No Fun

Doesn't it seem as if every day you are somehow reminded that "money makes the world go round"? It's lousy, but true. This is never more evident than when parents try to steer their youngsters toward appropriate institutions of higher learning. On the cover of *Cass and Birnbaum's Guide to American Colleges* (1996), the authors note four basic questions kids ask about college:

- Can I get in?
- Can I afford it?
- What will it be like when I get there?
- What kind of education will I receive?

Come to think of it, these four questions apply equally well to houses of ill repute. Never mind. Question number two is, for many parents, the biggie. Most folks want to send their child to the school with the best programs, best facilities, and most prestige. The money factor often limits their choices.

This chapter is devoted to three general categories of parents: (1) those who have to watch every penny, (2) those who can offer some financial help to their child, but not enough to cover all college expenses, and (3) parents who can afford any school their child wants. Parents in each of these categories have distinctly different perspectives on the funding issue. For the great majority, money talks and everything else walks.

17

Parents Looking for Funding

There are many ways to reduce the financial burden of college. First and foremost, *never, never, never pay out-of-state tuition!* Frugal parents must either get the college's officials to agree to in-state fee rates, or create some other strategy. For instance, you could have your aspiring student move to the state in which his or her college of choice is located and establish residence there first. (Make sure, however, that he or she can be admitted to the college before making this move. More information about the application and acceptance process follows in future chapters.) In most cases, establishing residence in a new state takes one year. (So he earns money and plays for a year; he's young, he won't mind.) Certain prestigious universities require two years to establish residence. It's worth noting that out-of-state tuition is normally *triple* the amount of in-state fees. If money is in short supply, this piece of advice is the most critical.

Next, consult with your son or daughter's high school counselor. Many high schools and local businesses offer first-year monies as rewards for various achievements in high school. Make sure your child knows about and has applied for these resources during his or her junior and senior years. They're going to claim to be too busy, so you really have to stay after them to get this one done. Follow-up phone calls to the school may be in order to insure that all possible grant and scholarship applications are on file.

Your child's high school counselor may also be a resource in obtaining other scholarships and grants. They often have the forms, phone numbers, and other resources right at their fingertips. Make your kid provide proof that he or she has talked to the counselor (it helps when they show some initiative). Afterward, a personal visit to the high school may be in order, to make sure all i's are dotted and all t's are crossed.

Following a visit with the high school counselor, you and your youngster will need to contact a university financial aid officer. Bear in mind that some collegiate financial assistance is generic, which means that the forms and processes will be the same, regardless of which school your new freshman chooses. Other funds are either state-specific or school-specific, and tailor-made application forms must be filled out.

The first step is to begin seeking federal assistance. Often, financially challenged families can get some help. Here's what the federal government has to offer.

Pell Grants. The best part about Pell Grants is that you don't have to pay back any money you get. The maximum amount is $2,300 per year, or 60 percent of annual college costs—whichever is lower. Financial need plays a major role in attaining these funds. Don't assume you aren't eligible: Ask!

Federal Supplemental Educational Opportunity Grants (FSEOG). These grants are also awarded based on financial need. The amount goes up to $4,000 per year. The place to begin learning about these grants is by writing or calling the U.S. Department of Education, U.S. Government Printing Office, Washington, D.C. 20402, Tel. 1-800-4 FED AID. Nearly every school will have additional information about them.

Federal Stafford Loans. (Also known as *Guaranteed Student Loans*.) These are loans on which interest is charged (though at a lower rate than prime). Stafford Loans up to $2,625 per year, are available to all students. Repayment terms are fairly manageable.

Federal Perkins Loans. These loans go up to $3,000 per year for five years, which totals a potential $15,000 in college dollars loaned to you at low interest. Repayment schedules extend as long as ten years after graduation. Both Stafford and Perkins loans help students build college fees into long-term budgets, meaning Mom and Dad won't have to foot the whole bill!

Federal Parent Loans. These loans (also known as *Plus Programs*) are for the amount needed to pay college expenses minus financial aid from other sources. Parents receive the funds but also have the repayment obligation.

Supplemental Loans for Students. These loans are for $4,000 during the first two years of school and $5,000 during the next two years. Students can defer payment of the principal, but not the interest, until after graduation.

Nellie Mae. The nation's largest nonprofit student-loan provider is called Nellie Mae. The organization is affiliated with CollegeView, a company that helps high school students tour campuses and pick out appropriate colleges to attend.

Badger the university financial aid officers to make certain you've applied for every form of assistance for which your family is eligible. Remember, they're being paid to provide this kind of service, so don't be shy. A personal visit is probably better than a phone call. (With voice-mail, they can easily avoid talking to you when you try to contact them by phone.) Besides, you want their undivided attention, which is more easily obtained in a face-to-face meeting. Your son or daughter should help with this effort. If your child just takes you for granted and assumes you'll do all the groundwork, he or she won't learn a valuable lesson in self-sufficiency, which this process could teach.

Besides grants and loans, the other key source of college funding comes from scholarships. These little pieces of financial heaven come from many places, including companies, unions, fraternal organizations, religious groups, state agencies, and groups representing various ethnic heritages. In addition, many benefactors have given monies to individual schools and universities to establish scholarships in their names for students with unique backgrounds or needs. There is an endless list of potential scholarship sources.

The key elements in gaining scholarships are the following:

- Entrance exam scores. American College Testing (ACT) and Scholastic Aptitude Test (SAT) scores are a major determining factor for many awards (you'll find more about these tests in chapter 3)
- Financial need
- Ethnic background or religious affiliation
- Athletic ability
- Musical skills
- Other academic qualifications

In addition, a wide variety of scholarships exists for special categories of students. For example, older students, international students, students with disabilities, and gifted students often receive scholarships based on these qualifying characteristics. Now, more than ever before, college access is not limited to the privileged.

Most scholarships require specific application procedures. Written inquiries regarding specific scholarships may be used to make the initial contact. School officials should help you fill out the actual application form, especially if your son or daughter has been admitted to the college. It is essential to meet submission deadlines and to document all accomplishments and eligibility factors that might help gain a scholarship or award. For further information, you may wish to read *Cash for College: The Ultimate Guide for College Scholarships* (1993).

The federal government requires students needing financial help to fill out a form known as the Free Application for Federal Student Aid (FAFSA). Individual colleges often require another document, known as the Financial Aid Form (FAF). The information you provide helps school officials lead you toward appropriate scholarship opportunities.

As mentioned, the bulk of freshmen scholarships are tied to high school grades and ACT or SAT scores, or are based on special abilities, such as in music, art, or sports. Many colleges offer other grants and funds from unusual sources, so try hard to investigate every available possibility. Don't give up. Dig, search, study, and ask questions. You never know where you might discover an unexpected source of money.

Once the student has completed the freshman year of college, you should reexamine all of the scholarship possibilities. Many schools offer additional funds to those who have done well in the first two years and have moved on to a specific major. Parents and their children may lose out by not seeking out new scholarships and grants each year. Your kid is again going to say he or she is too busy to find these opportunities, so be proactive and help out. If that doesn't work, threaten not to pay the next tuition bill if he doesn't make the effort to seek out these additional sources of financial assistance.

Parents who have low incomes must try diligently to obtain financing for college. Establish a partnership with your son or daughter. Instead of lack of sufficient money being something to fight about, make it a challenge to overcome together. Finding funding is no fun. Getting funding is a blast!

Parents Who Need a Boost

Many of you may already have set aside a few dollars in a college fund. Unfortunately, for many years the cost of university education has been increasing at a rate far greater than inflation. This may leave you in the position of being able to help, but not completely able to cover the entire cost of college for your child. If this is your situation, most of the advice provided in the previous section applies to you.

Both financially strapped parents and those who can offer some assistance to their children should seek a commitment from their kids to contribute toward college expenses. One way to accomplish this is to encourage your son or daughter to apply for on-campus employment. Many departments hire clerical workers. Food services hire kitchen and counter help. Numerous other job possibilities exist as well. For many, a twenty-hour-per-week workload can be managed, and those few extra dollars are ones you won't have to come up with. She gains a sense of accomplishment from earning her own spending money and from managing a busier schedule.

Remember the ever-possible G.I. Bill. Young adults who have the proper temperament may benefit from spending a few years in the military. Enlistment can generate a considerable number of dollars for college, and provide opportunities for maturing and learning *before* school starts. It's not a bad way to go for many kids who need to grow up a little bit before entering college. If nothing else, military service teaches discipline, structure, and goal setting— three key skills which are great assets in a college environment.

Also for the militarily-minded, Reserve Officers' Training Corps (ROTC) programs are a great way to pick up college cash. Sure, males have to sport funny haircuts, and both genders are forced to wear fatigues on certain school days. At the same time, bonding, friendships, and funding are part of ROTC experience. Besides, most ROTC programs require a couple of years of active duty after college, which means the participant won't be wondering what to do after graduation. In general, when Uncle Sam picks up the tab, Mom and Dad don't have to pay! Thus, you may want to mention these options to your youngster, especially if he or she is having a hard time getting focused on school (or life).

Even if scholarships or grants are obtained, you probably will still need to cushion the financial blow caused by the part of the college costs you actually have to pay. Here are some of the things the school's financial aid officer will either offer or suggest:

- Make regular installment payments—a plan offered by most schools—so that fees are built into your regular cash flow
- Obtain financing, usually from a bank, to spread out the payments over a series of years
- You could use a charge card
- Use a home equity loan to spread out the payments, making the interest tax-deductible
- Let your kid deal with it
- Cash all those old savings bonds that were saved for a rainy day. (This is a rainy day!)

Getting cooperation from someone eighteen to twenty years old, in the area of fiscal responsibility, is not easy. Arguments will arise, and your son or daughter will probably want you to handle everything. These touchy negotiations demand your concern and careful deliberation. (First you may need a 2x4 to get their attention!) While working out a financial agreement, it's important to consider these thoughts as you struggle to find a balance with your new college student:

- What percentage of my income do I intend to forgo to help him pay for college? Will I reach or exceed that amount?
- Does my child need to *learn a lesson* by working, or is college life merely an extension of what she did in high school?
- Is my child frugal or frivolous?
- How much am I willing to pay simply to keep my kid out of the house and out of my hair?
- Do I sound like my mother or father when I talk to him about money? Does it make me wince to know that I do?
- Does she hear anything of what I say when I talk about money?
- Is there even a chance that some day he or she will make it big and buy me a house out of gratitude? If yes, shouldn't I fork over a few dollars now, just as an insurance policy?

Of course, if you're lucky enough to have a daughter or son who really wants to help, you should be prepared to suggest ways they can earn money without interfering with academic work. Flexible options, such as self-employment providing services (typing papers, cleaning houses, doing yard work) may be better than regular part-time employment.

Working While in School

Remember the Psych 101 class you took in college (or in high school)? Were you taught about approach-avoidance conflicts? Life is an approach-avoidance conflict. Everything good seems to come attached to something bad. Good things can arise from bad events. So it is with a college student who is employed, full- or part-time.

The upside of working your way through college includes a few things briefly mentioned earlier. A sense of self-sufficiency comes from earning some of your own keep. Part-time employment forces the aspiring collegian to prioritize, organize, and, in general, become a better time manager. It can even, in some rare instances, make a young person be a little more careful with cash, spending less lavishly and foolishly. Self-confidence, self-reliance, and a sense of accomplishment can be a part of college-age employment.

The downside of working while in school is that things sometimes get out of balance. Students sometimes overvalue work and neglect classes. Moreover, the odds are great that your child will simply blow the money, becoming a slave to fashion and to an expensive lifestyle. Admittedly this is an accurate replica of later life, but still, why should they start so soon? In some cases, clashes with coworkers can carry over to the campus and become unnecessary distractions. Not good. Worst of all, some students like working, and the money associated with it, so well that they want to drop out of school, mortgaging their long-term future in exchange for looking good at a few weekend parties or on a few dates.

As a parent, your job is to balance these pros and cons, taking into account your child's spending history and other past tendencies regarding money. The original bargain that you strike regarding college funding, employment, and other money issues may not be the same one that exists in later years. At first, simply work out a deal everyone can live with. There will be plenty of time for additional conflict later!

When Money Is No Object

It would be nice if everyone could be in this category, especially when it comes to selecting a college. Unfortunately, only a limited number of parents have the luxury of not needing to concern themselves about college costs. Those who don't have money problems find other factors are more relevant. Which criteria rise to the surface when finances are not the key ingredient? In general, as parents, you should try to see to it that the major factors considered by your child in selecting a college include:

- prestige of the school
- whether or not the institution will admit the student
- the quality and range of academic programs
- personality fit with the school (see chapter 3)
- travel costs and time needed to get home
- opportunities for extracurricular activities

In certain regions of the country, it is more likely that your son or daughter will encounter a gauntlet of roadblocks, called *screening devices* or something similar. It helps if Mom and Dad can realistically assess which schools are likely to accept their child. *Barron's Profiles of American Colleges—Northeast* (1994) actually categorizes universities and schools into (1) most competitive, (2) highly competitive, (3) competitive, (4) marginally competitive, and (5) not competitive. You and your youngster together should decide which level of school he or she will seek to enter. You want to aim as high as possible without creating a situation where only frustration and rejection result.

It is probably a good idea to downplay the "snob factor" when helping your child select potential colleges to attend. The most important thing is to be certain that the school matches with his or her personality and interests. Then, to raise your odds of success, be sure to document all the awards, experiences, and accomplishments that will be considered during the admissions process. (See chapter 3 for more details.)

In many cases, moving away from home will increase your child's chances of being admitted at a prestigious or quality institution. Many university administrators seek to develop a student body with as much geographic diversity as possible. They also look for well-rounded kids who, at the same time, have one or two special gifts or talents, in art, music, theater, debate, sports, or other areas. Anything you can do to encourage your child's participation in *high school* activities may help when it comes time to apply for college.

Even when money is not the major factor in the choice of a school, parents should seek out scholarships for which their daughters or sons are entitled. These awards are good selling points on post-college résumés and lessen your expenses at the same time. You still will be negotiating matters such as whether the student will work at a job she or he may want to earn some spending money. Some schools require on-campus employment or unpaid community-service activity in order for students to receive certain scholarships or grants. These involvements can be a useful part of the learning process (time-management skills are sharpened, for example).

Choosing Your Poison

Generating and maintaining a financial plan for coping with college expenses is a tough chore. For parents who have no idea how to get started, be reminded that high school counselors and college or university financial aid officers are a good place to start. Also, many websites have been created to help with this process. If you are old-fashioned when it comes to computers, there are numerous books available to help you learn about them. At the end of this chapter is a list of a few other resources that may help you find funds.

Meanwhile, recognize the potential landmines that accompany discussions with your kids about money. To whatever degree is possible, reassure him or her that you are trying to help. Many high school seniors believe Mom and Dad simply want to run their lives and lord over them with the checkbook. Such an approach is counterproductive for both parents and students. If you can, disarm your son or daughter's fears and try to create a more adult-to-adult partnership as you seek money for college. Let your kid know you want him to be happy with his choice, and to feel that the college he selects is the best alternative possible—not just a compromise. There is a long journey ahead, beginning with narrowing down to a few finalists the more than ten thousand options (the number of colleges and universities in the United States) and then being accepted by a desired school. It's still early in the game, but survival depends on reaching a financial arrangement that everyone can accept. Good luck.

Read More About It

Printed Resources

Barron's Profiles of American Colleges—Northeast. 11th ed. Hauppauge, NY: Barron's Educational Series, Inc., 1994.

Cass & Birnbaum's Guide to American Colleges. 6th ed. New York: HarperPerennial, 1996.

Dennis, Marguerite J. *Barron's Complete College Financing Guide,* 3d ed. Hauppauge, NY: Barron's Educational Series, Inc., 1994.

Deutschman, Alan. *Winning Money for College—The High School Student's Guide to Scholarship Contests.* 3d ed. Princeton, NJ: Peterson's Guides, 1992.

The Princeton Review Student Access Guide to Paying for College. 1996 edition. New York: Random House, 1996.

Ragins, Marianne. *Winning Scholarships for College: An Insider's Guide.* New York: Henry Holt, 1994.

Ruiz, McKee, Cynthia, and Phillip C. McKee, Jr. *Cash for College: The Ultimate Guide for College Scholarships.* New York: Hearst Books, 1993.

Electronic Resources

http://www.collegeview.com
http://www.nelliemae.org
http://www.ed.gov/offices/OPE/express.html (for FAFSA form)

3

Applications and Aggravations

In a perfect world, your son or daughter would be able to do a low-key, careful survey of every potentially suitable college or university at a leisurely pace. The world of college admissions, however, is not even close to perfect. First of all, each application package that you and your kid send out costs both time and money. There are forms to complete, high school transcripts to request, essays to write, and fees to pay. Each school will charge somewhere between $20 and $200 (even more at elite colleges) just to apply, and still reserve the right to reject the application! Makes you mad just thinking about it, doesn't it? Application is aggravation. Your child can get discouraged pretty easily. It's your job to help him or her narrow down the field to some finalists, and then send in the application forms. A few pointers about these activities may help you survive with a less grim outlook on the basic goodness of human nature.

Trying to select a college is a two-way street. To the student, the street looks more like a drawbridge over a moat filled with alligators and snakes. That's because many schools have rather imposing screening devices.

From the university's perspective, the goal is to generate a student body filled with energetic, hardworking, qualified students who will go forth after graduation and make the institution look good. Troublemakers and other undesirables must be carefully weeded out. Consequently all students and parents must present a positive case for admission.

Several factors tend to shape the selection process as it is designed by each school. These factors may also be predictors of the eventual success (or failure) of your young scholar, both in terms of successfully applying to the school and subsequent achievements while there. A few ingredients stand out. On a more-or-less philosophical level, one element you should consider is how well a student will fit in at a specific university.

Types of Schools

Just as different people have different temperaments, individual universities have particular personalities. Sharon G. Johnson (while a professor at Baylor University) wrote an article in which he categorized colleges as being one of four kinds: (1) factories, (2) families, (3) foundries, and (4) fairs. Take a close look at the schools you're investigating, and these attributes should become evident.

A *factory* is a college or university that cranks out graduates with readily identifiable skills and educational accomplishments, because all students take the same classes, which are directly related to marketplace demands. An anonymous faculty member from one of these institutions once remarked, "We are the Wal-Mart of colleges in this area." In other words, his was a low-cost, ready-to-go-to-work, practical-education outlet, where graduates were "manufactured" with numbing uniformity. There's nothing wrong with that, as long as your child wants to be a square peg that fits a square hole. Many nontraditional students love factories, because they get in and out in short order and quickly learn tailor-made job skills.

Families are the hug-'em-and-love-'em places mentioned in chapter 1. The school serves as an extended nuclear family, complete with parents (faculty), siblings (fellow students), and even kindly aunts and uncles (counselors and tutors). Small colleges and jucos are often of the family variety. Some departments within large universities operate in the same manner. Not every twenty-year-old wants to be hugged and loved, however, so make sure your daughter or son knows how the college is going to work.

Foundries build and mold high-powered individuals. Students are taught and images are created based on intense mentoring by a key faculty member. The body of knowledge associated with that professor is offered to the student. The Citadel, the Air Force Academy, the U.S. Military Academy at West Point, and other military schools are foundries. Many church colleges function as foundries, especially those with preseminary programs. There is an upside and a downside to a foundry. The upside is that you may end up with a college senior with strength of character or values that will make him or her the next George Washington or Colin Powell. The downside is that you may end up with a college senior in the vein of G. Gordon Liddy or Jim Baker. It takes a unique individual to conquer the rigors of the foundry. The person must be strong-willed, talented, and self-motivated in order to thrive.

Fairs are the all-things-to-all-people schools. These schools are like fairgrounds where one can walk along, picking and choosing from a variety of courses, programs, majors, and paths. It takes a certain kind of focus to seek out the right classes in fairs. On the other hand, those who are going to school to simply sample the knowledge available, those who have a job lined up in the family business and don't need to worry about specialized knowledge, and those who have a general interest in learning but not necessarily in getting a diploma are highly suited to this model.

None of the four prototypes is good or bad. They are simply different. As a parent you'll want to encourage your son or daughter to select places that match his or her needs and preferences. It may be helpful to pick out five to ten schools that seem to interest your kid, and see if they fit into one of these categories. Understanding the relative benefits of each type may help you and your child narrow down the list of potential campuses to choose. In addition, placement services, especially at colleges that do not have *open enrollment* (a policy of admitting anyone with a high school diploma), try to make certain a good fit exists between student and school.

One piece of advice offered by many sources is essentially: Know thyself. Only the young person in question can truly assess which things matter the most when selecting a type of school. Listing the five most important things a school can offer might help you and them decide on a general type of college or university to investigate. Make sure your youngster considers things like preferences for small-town or big-city living, college size, living arrangements (see chapters 8 and 9), and involvement levels. In smaller schools, it's easier to be involved in a variety of activities than it is in larger colleges. If your kid is a social climber in the making, school prestige and name value are going to be crucial factors. No matter which selection criteria are listed, those factors should figure heavily in your analysis of potential schools to contact.

Your child holds the keys to many of the other factors that affect the choice of a school. These include college entrance exams, high school grades, and the other tests and screens established by the system. Each factor contributes mightily to the decisions made by a school admissions officer regarding the incoming freshman class.

Entrance Exams

For many kids, the most noteworthy screening device is going to be his or her ACT (American College Testing) or SAT (Scholastic Aptitude Test) score. Nearly every institution in the United States uses one or both of these exams. These tests help determine who gets in, who gets scholarships, and which classes some students must take, especially in the first year.

A variety of high-quality study guides are available on the market. Some of them are listed at the end of this chapter. In addition, there are courses students can take to help prepare for the exams. Getting ready for college-entrance exams is a major subject that your son or daughter should study and learn about—the sooner the better.

For the purposes of this book, a small amount of information is being presented to provide a background. First, to give you a sense of what "normal" is, the median score (or 50th percentile) on the ACT is about 20, based on a range of 1–36. The median mark on the SAT, where scores range from 200–800, is 510.

An ACT score of 25 or above, or an SAT score of 650 or above, in either the verbal or math categories, is cause for celebration. These numbers normally will make a student eligible for academic scholarships and other resources. A score of 30 or more on the ACT or a 710 on the SAT calls for a major party, since such figures typically generate big-time money, up to and including *free rides* (tuition-free enrollment). In fact, some states offer "Bright Flight" funding, which is an annual cash payment to the best-scoring high school seniors. The payments are designed to keep highly intelligent local scholars in a given state's university system. It is possible, at this level, to actually make money by going to college. Before you get delusions of grandeur about your kid, however, be advised that these scores are achieved less than than one percent of the time.

At the other end of the spectrum, an ACT score of 14 or less, or a score of 390 of less on the SAT, may keep your child from being admitted to most colleges *except* for open-admissions institutions. Open-admissions policies are in place at many junior colleges, some small colleges, and certain regional colleges and universities, as well as at several land-grant universities in the Midwest.

Low SAT or ACT scores will mean that the student will end up in what are called *remedial* classes. And yes, it's true, some people call these courses "bonehead math" and "bonehead English." Don't be too discouraged by low tallies, or by your child being placed in remedial classes. The classes are designed to help him or her to catch up and get prepared for studies at a higher level. Besides, everyone knows that admissions tests are culturally biased, which means that some minorities may not fare well on them, because of cultural differences, incomplete fluency in the English language, or lack of preparation in some areas. More importantly, marginal students can and do graduate from college every year. Interest, effort, intensity, and *attendance* make a huge difference. Tutoring and other widely available services have been created to assist disadvantaged students.

Read carefully the information package that will accompany your child's admission-test results. It will offer hints regarding where your daughter or son stands relative to other high school students. Sometimes a list of careers and majors that match your youngster's interests and abilities will be provided. Scores achieved previously on high school aptitude tests, such as the MMAT (Minnesota Multiphasic Aptitude Test) provide additional information regarding their most viable choices of majors in college and of subsequent careers.

High School Grades

Like it or not—and most high school kids don't like it—grades do have meaning. Admittance to college depends in part on high school grades. Class rank, as determined by marks in high school, is an important element in determining eligibility for some colleges. Grades also affect decisions about allocating scholarships and grants. School officials normally create a mystical formula, using grades combined with SAT scores, to determine which seniors are selected for entrance into the institution.

Most colleges convert high school grades to the 4.0 scale, where all A's become 4.0; B's, 3; C's, 2; D's, 1; and F's get zeroes. These grades are used to calculate a grade point average (GPA). The GPA may be multiplied by the SAT or ACT score to yield an overall score. Then the school establishes a cutoff point.

Some universities use class rank rather than grades to make the determination. Either way, those of you who bought this book wondering how to help your child get into college must accept this fact: *When it comes to grades, it's too late!*

By the senior year in high school, the die already has been cast on the grade point front. Fortunately, many college choices are available, and your youngster gets a clean slate once college courses begin—so don't fret about what you can't fix. Identify the options that are realistic and pick from those.

Other Screening Devices

The most bizarre selection or screening device used by institutions of higher learning is the entrance examination essay. What are these college officials thinking? It's their job to teach students how to write at an advanced level, yet they want evidence of this skill before the kid even starts! Is that fair? It seems comparable to asking someone to take a preliminary driver's test, to see if he has a driving aptitude. Ridiculous. Even the most unimaginative administrator (and there's plenty of competition in that arena) should be able to figure out who actually does the writing—the parents! Table 3.1 provides a sampling of what might happen if the kids actually were left to complete this task.

TABLE 3.1

Typical College Entrance Exam Questions and Answers

Question: Where do you want to be in twenty years?

What they write: "I plan to be in my most productive career years and will be moving on to the mentoring and coaching stage, where I help others coming up through the ranks."

The real answer: "I want to be on my private yacht, sunbathing and hanging out with my friends."

Question: What kinds of experiences have you had that will aid you in college?

What they write: "My time as president of the Key Club helped me learn leadership, working at the homeless shelter taught me compassion, and the basketball squad taught me teamwork."

The real answer: "I learned how to chug a beer at a party last summer. What else do I need to know?"

Question: Describe your special interests, and how you intend to pursue them in college.

What they write: "Playing in the pep band or orchestra will help me pursue my interest in music. Working on the school newspaper or yearbook will allow me to explore my interest in writing. And, who knows what new interests I will develop with such a rich array of possibilities offered by your institution?" (which is a real suck-up response)

The real answer: "I once dated three different people in one week. In college, I'd like to go for four."

Question: What is your favorite book, or who is your favorite author?

What they write: "Tolstoy; Nietzsche; and John Grisham for lighter reading."

The real answer: (Males) "*How to Pick Up Women*, Madonna's *Sex*, and *The Joy of Sex, Illustrated, Volume 2*." (Females) "Danielle Steele novels and *People Magazine's 100 Most Eligible Bachelors*."

Question: Describe a current event and how it affected you.

What they write: "The most recent peace initiative in the Middle East

gave me the hope that one day all humanity will live in harmony. The
most recent election restored my faith in the democratic system. And,
a firefighter rescued a kitten from a tree, reminding me that all life is
precious."
The real answer: "My most recent CD purchase really moved me."

Question: Describe an influential person who has affected your life.
What they write: "Gandhi, who taught civil disobedience; Martin
Luther King, who taught courage and compassion; and Abraham
Lincoln, who taught about equality."
The real answer: "Jenny, who taught me about French kissing."

Question: What is your objective in college?
What they write: "To get a meaningful degree, to start a meaningful
career, to help other people."
The real answer: "To learn something easy that will make me a whole
bunch of money real fast."

Question: Name an accomplishment or achievement of which you are
proud.
What they write: "Making the honor roll, winning the 4–H pie-baking
contest, and my Sunday school attendance record.
The real answer: "Climbing out the back window, staying out all night,
and not getting caught by my parents, even though I was exhausted
all day. They never had a clue!"

Question: How do you feel about the present, and how do you feel
about the future?
What they write: "Now I am happy to be entering this exciting new
phase of my life. The future is filled with unlimited promise."
The real answer: "Now I am fed up with these stupid questions, and
later I'm going to hang out with my friends at the mall."

The scariest moment comes when a question, such as "Who are
you?" seems to baffle your youngster, and the kid replies, "I'm not
sure." It's also disturbing if, when asked, "What is the most exciting
thing in your life?" he or she responds, "I don't really have a life."

The whole essay process, then, is a matter of fiction writing—not exactly a primary talent needed for anything but maybe English 101. Still, somebody actually does read the answers.

As a result, parents end up doing the writing, or coaching their kid so much that they might as well be doing the writing. At least one college has finally understood what truly happens and simply asks the parents to write the essay directly. Now *that's* a victory of reality over hypocrisy.

In any case, these essays may partially determine not just who gains admission to the school, but also who wins individual scholarships. Consequently, parents have to take them seriously. There are several guides for writing entrance essays, including the excellent chapter on "Writing Great Essays" in *The Admissions Essay: How to Stop Worrying and Start Writing* (1987) and *The Parents' Guide to Surviving the College Admissions Process* (1996), both from Citadel Press, the same fine folks who are bringing you this book. Buy the books, be prepared, and do all you can to get your son or daughter into a preferred school, with as much financial help as possible!

Taking Action

Finally, you need to sit down with your youngster and spell out a list of colleges he or she wants to consider closely. It's a good idea to narrow your prospect list down to nine to twelve places. Put three or four schools into each of these categories:

- "Places I want to try, but which may be out of my league."
- "Places I'm pretty sure will admit me, and would really make me happy if they did."
- "Places where I know I will be accepted, and can use as final fallbacks if necessary."

Early in your son or daughter's senior year this list should start taking on a final form, because soon they'll need to fill out the necessary paperwork. It won't be long until some schools fall off the list, for financial, scholarly, or logistical reasons. You will end up paying some application fees that yield no results. Just consider those dollars as an investment in reclaiming control of your house.

Be advised that some schools now allow you to apply via the Internet or by sending in a disk. Many kids like this approach, as it gives them a chance to play on a computer while doing something constructive. Whatever works is what you want. Just make sure they follow through and send off the correct information.

Once the applications are on their way, two things follow. The first is the classic game of "hurry up and wait." There is a mad dash to get all the papers filed on time, and then it seems as if you wait forever to get a reply. Second, when you do hear back, it's usually from a college recruiter or admissions counselor, who asks you to bring your kid around for a visit. Your task is to make certain your kid keeps track of the invitations and of the other schools he or she wants to visit. Then you can help create a schedule to visit the final candidates.

The final selection of a college is going to be a significant decision. If a college chosen by your youngster responds in kind (by choosing to admit your son or daughter), you have passed the first hurdle. Sometimes this obstacle is quite small. For example, policies of most land-grant universities declare that any student who has graduated from an in-state high school is eligible to at least give college a try. In other cases a major sense of triumph results from gaining admission to an academically or socially prestigious institution. Whatever the case, there are still a few more tasks to complete before the final choice is made. If you thought the application process was aggravating, just wait until you've visited the campus!

References

Berger, Larry, et al. *Up Your Score: The Underground Guide to the SAT.* New York: Workman Publishing, 1996.

Dalby, Sidonia and Sally Rubenstone. *College Admissions: A Crash Course for Panicked Parents.* New York: Macmillan, 1994.

Fitzpatrick, Ellen Pinkman, and Barbara Trecher. *The Parents' Guide to Surviving the College Admissions Process.* Secaucus, NJ: Citadel Press, 1996.

Hayden, Thomas C. *Peterson's Handbook for College Admission,* 4th ed. Princeton, NJ: Peterson's, 1995.

Johnson, Sharon G. "College Business Education: Some Irreverent Images, With Not So Irreverent Consequences." In *Proceedings*, 69–72. 1983. Southwest Academy of Management Meeting, Houston, Texas.

Kaplan's ACT All-in-One. New York: Simon and Schuster, 1996.

Power, Helen, and Robert DiAn. *The Admissions Essay: How to Stop Worrying and Start Writing*. Secaucus, NJ: Citadel Press, 1996.

Robinson, Adam, and John Katzman. *The Princeton Review: Cracking the SAT and PSAT*. New York: Random House, 1997.

4

Campus Visits

College recruiters know that the courtship process is the lifeblood of their institutions. This makes them relentless, almost pushy, under the thin veneer of being nice folks. They aren't quite in the same league as used-car salesmen, but may be at least distant relatives. It's wise to bear in mind that individual careers in student recruiting are made or broken based on the capricious choices of seventeen- and eighteen-year-olds. Talk about pressure! Burnout rates are huge.

Normally, a college or university will annually take three or four of their most bright-eyed graduates, especially the ones who had great times during their college careers, and turn them into traveling recruiters. At the end of three years, maybe only one remains on the job. The constant journeys and continual disappointments wear down the others. Fortunately for the school, each year brings a new batch of these kinds of eternal (temporarily) optimists.

School recruiters are the ones who will arrange campus visits for you and your son or daughter. The toughest part of making plans may be staying in touch, because recruiters spend a great deal of time on the road, visiting high schools and prospective students. This means it's up to you to make sure on-campus interviews and visits yield the kinds of information and insights they should, for both you and your child.

The campus visit is often a key ingredient in the final choice of a school. The potential student observes, firsthand, college life in all its glory. To keep them from being too wide-eyed or becoming dazed by all they see, you need to help them stay focused on the task at hand, which is picking the right college to attend.

Parents can adopt one of several strategies when it comes time to pay a visit to the university. Some folks stay home, for one or more of the following reasons:

- Mom and Dad are simply too busy and can't make the trip, even if they want to go along
- The child, in a bold move toward independence, announces he or she wants to make the journey alone
- The parents believe it would be a better learning experience for the kid to go alone
- You've just had a series of disastrous family vacations and figure a campus visit would turn out the same way
- The prospective student is so undecided that Mom and Dad want a firmer commitment before investing their own time in a trip

Whatever the case, sending an eighteen-year-old high school senior off to a strange campus can be a risky approach. Some kids are so insecure that they will hide throughout the visit and never ask the kinds of key questions that would help them make an informed decision about attending a particular college. Others abuse the system, make a whole series of trips just to get out of high school, and goof around the entire time, sneaking away to places like the nearest video arcade and McDonald's rather than actually touring the campus. There are other young people who are quite sincere about their interest in a place, but simply don't know what kinds of questions to ask, and may fail to think about the things that will truly matter to them in the next four years.

As a result, if your intention is to send your child on campus visits alone, you need to carefully prepare him or her for the journey. This means helping make a list of questions to ask, as well as an itinerary of places to go and people to see. Young people with special talents, whether in athletics, music, journalism, photography, debating, or something else, need to make certain an appointment is scheduled with the key faculty member who will help them develop the skill, or who will make the decision about a scholarship based on the specific talent. Ordinarily, coaches and athletic programs have the most finely tuned approach to campus visits, because of NCAA (National Collegiate Athletic Association) regulations. Music programs are probably a close second. Other schools and departments may not be quite as well prepared to roll out the red carpet for any particular youngster.

Before the trip, instruct your son or daughter to bring back lots of printed matter, such as catalogs, application forms, descriptions of majors, and financial aid packages. Also demand that they return with phone numbers and addresses (business cards are good) of the people they spoke with during their visit. E-mail addresses are a great way to talk to some professors and recruiters. Only with high-quality preparation will your son or daughter gain the fullest benefit from a campus visit.

Your child may want to take along a friend, which may not be a bad idea, as friends might ask questions that would otherwise not be posed. If the two are truly interested in a specific university, it can work out pretty well. If not, they'll just goof around and you'll lose out on some travel money. At that point your kid is simply playing a high-class form of hooky.

When Mom or Dad Goes Along

Making a road trip with a high school senior is almost always an adventure. Simply agreeing on a day to make the visit is a major task. Then, he wants to drive. Or, she wants to blare the radio so loud it stirs up your tinnitus. They will want fast food, and your kids will want you to pay for everything. If things go normally, before you even reach the campus, you're already annoyed! Just being in a car for a long time with your kid, when you're not used to it, can make for a hard ride.

Do the best you can to avoid these pitfalls. Establish some ground rules before you start. One great tactic is to take along an innocent bystander, like a grandparent, who will cause your son or daughter to be on better behavior. Let your child know in advance whether he or she will get to take the wheel. Plan stops carefully, so everyone gets what they need. Then, load up the car and off you go (unless, of course, you're flying—then you need to negotiate carry-on-luggage-versus-checking-bags issues).

Once you reach campus, a brightly smiling recruiter will greet you with a schedule of events designed to optimize the school's chances of making a positive impression on both you and your child.

How does it work? Truthfully, it's a simple process. They will show the kids one thing and the parents another. Parents are ordinarily interested in:

- facilities and classrooms
- programs and majors
- faculty credentials
- the *student–faculty ratio*, which gives you a sense of the potential size of individual classes
- funding, scholarships, and grants
- student support services

On the other hand, prospective students are more likely to seek out:

- the video gameroom in the student union
- information about extracurricular activities
- campus beauty (or the opposite-gender variety)
- and, more positively, the availability of computer facilities

Therefore, the first thing you, as a parent, should understand is that your child's experiences during a campus visit are completely different from yours. Recruiters will carefully take you to one place and your son or daughter to another (in much the same way that the police immediately separate suspects at a crime scene). You'll get cookies and punch or coffee. They'll get pizza and coke. You'll be introduced to Dr. This, along with Professor That, and possibly even to Dean or President So and So. They'll be introduced to Buffy and Matt.

Just as a horse requires blinders to keep on a straight path, parents must focus their children on the task at hand. So, even if they fail to solicit useful information, you should. Questions parents should ask include:

- Does this school offer majors that my son or daughter is interested in? Does the school's program in that area have a good reputation?
- Does this school have a solid placement program for its graduates?
- What percentage of the college's graduates actually get jobs in their chosen fields?
- How much help will the student get in completing the degree program? What kind of help?

Some colleges, especially those experiencing declining enrollments, make a grand effort to make their institution seem desirable. This means they will generate a whole day's worth of activities for you to endure.

A typical program begins with an address by an administrator. He or she tells a terrible joke, which is followed by some uncomfortable laughter, and then begins a speech that causes your mind to wander so quickly that you immediately suspect you're in for a long day.

Soon afterward, the recruiters, school counselors, and other campus officials go to work. They'll tell you about parking, security, registration, due dates for fees, deadlines for applications, programs, grades, academic probation, and school rules, and will give a flood of other information you actually can use. Pay attention, take notes, ask questions, and pick up as many handouts as they give, so you can study them later. This is one time when school personnel work really hard to keep you happy. Once they've got your kid reeled in, things change—so take advantage of this opportunity.

Many colleges will also trot out the school band, swing choir, a speaker, or a theater performance to impress and entertain you. These students serve to display the kinds of skills your child may develop while in school. In truth, all the other students on campus probably hate these little showboats. So, just enjoy the performance for what it is.

At lunch you will sample food that is never served in the school cafeteria. The university couldn't afford it.

Sooner or later, a campus ambassador, most likely a junior or senior, will take you on a tour. You usually can ask more direct questions of them, about parties, drinking, toughness of classes, and other issues that may be either distracting to or frustrating for your child down the road. Often these students are more willing to talk to you directly about school pros and cons. If it seems they are, go ahead and ask these trickier questions.

At some point you will rendezvous with your son or daughter. Make sure all their questions have been answered as well. Try to keep them focused on important issues, like academics and activities. School recruiters are most interested in seeing that your kid has a fun campus visit. It's your job to see that everything else gets accomplished.

Finally, it's time to head for home. Some colleges have overnight programs for visiting students. Probably not a whole lot is gained by the extended stays, so treat them with a certain amount of indifference.

Once you are back home, sit down and draw up a list of advantages and problems you noticed at each school. Talk with your youngster to see if the experience either excited or discouraged him or her. Because all the prospects can blur together in your mind, photos, brochures, notes, and other memory aids may help you sort things out later.

There is one other approach to campus visits, which is to go on your own. If your daughter makes the trip without notifying the administration, she can wander around without someone looking over her shoulder the whole time. Just hanging out at a campus can be highly instructive.

Another good alternative is to arrange a visit with a friend who already attends the school, again without announcing the visit to school officials. These visits can give your kid a sense of a school's ambience in a totally unedited fashion.

Interviews and Auditions

A few elite schools may call your child back for an actual interview. Make sure he or she dresses appropriately, prepares a list of questions to ask, and thinks about answers to their questions, which will be similar to the ones posed for admissions essays. The interview is a process in which your child should try to make a good enough impression on the admissions committee so that he or she will be selected. For some kids, it's a critical moment. Being rejected after being interviewed is going to be hard to endure. You may be called upon to render some big-time emotional reassurance and ego-bolstering if that occurs. Be ready to respond to your youngster's success *or* failure after the interview takes place.

The same holds true for kids who must try out for a scholarship by playing a musical instrument or performing in some other way. These high-anxiety sessions determine who gets a scholarship and affect the odds of acceptance in some universities. Mom and Dad should see their roles as supportive, helping calm down their child so he or she can perform effectively, and giving praise for the effort, no matter how things turn out. You should be an ally when your child is being asked to "put up or shut up" as a college applicant.

As the autumn of the senior year of high school advances, it's time to get serious. Strongly encourage your youngster to narrow down the options to about three top candidates. Send a completed application package to each, including scholarship requests, transcripts, application forms, financial aid forms, letters of recommendation, and all other materials requested. Fairly soon, it will be crunch time. Choosing a school is never easy. As you might expect, this means more trauma in your future. Don't give up. It won't be long until the choice is made, and your youngster actually heads off to begin the freshman year. At that point, all these up-front costs will suddenly seem well worth the investment of your time and money. It's a leap of faith to believe it at this point, but there *is* a light at the end of the recruiting tunnel!

5

The Choice

The decision to matriculate (a fancy word for "enroll") at an institution of higher learning is based on numerous elements. Sometimes a factor as simple as the beauty of the campus makes the difference. The persuasiveness of the recruiter may also play a key role. To the prospective new student, this four-or-more-year commitment is one of the most significant he or she has made since deciding about ear-piercing.

Parents are sometimes able to influence their child's thinking during the process of choosing a school. Mom and Dad should not make the decision, however. The kid has to live with whatever she selects, so give her some room. Remember, making a choice can be traumatic, which means parents will bear the brunt of their child's anxiety. Here are some issues to think about as things progress.

Things to Watch Out For

First and foremost, there are some pitfalls to avoid during the selection of a school. These potential errors can easily be made by youngsters as they are being recruited, and parents are sorely tested when they arise.

Delusions of Grandeur. Your child's first choice of school is likely to be based on the belief that he or she is Harvard or Princeton material, or destined for some other prestigious, pricey place. Most of the time these beliefs are unrealistic. In this case, it is your job to bring your child back to earth and reality without crushing an ego or seeming to be a money-grubbing penny-pincher who doesn't care about her future. That's a tough one. (Of course, if she actually is Harvard or Princeton material, you're in an even more difficult predicament. For one thing, you're probably going to have to mortgage your house to pay tuition.)

For the fortunate few parents who can afford any place their child wants, there are other delusions of grandeur to address. To begin with, being *admitted* is not the same thing as *graduating*. Sometimes kids forget they actually have to do things like show up for class and work hard. It's your task to provide them with the occasional reality check, so they will be ready to face the tasks ahead. Also, a young person can let an institution's name and reputation go to his head fairly easily. Unless you don't mind getting snobbery and egotistical one-upmanship from your youngster, you'll have to work on convincing him that school is an opportunity rather than a birthright.

The Mismatch. Another problem is that your child's boyfriend or girlfriend is likely to have a decisive impact on the choice made by your new collegian. Unfortunately, what's right for a partner may not be the best for your son or daughter who picks a school based on puppy love rather than rational thought. For parents, this experience is similar to the dilemma you encounter when your daughter brings home a future Hell's Angel. Make a big deal about her lack of judgment and you might as well start writing out wedding invitations or forming elopement explanations on the spot.

The best way to deal with the college-togetherness issue is to point out how close your son or daughter can be to that significant other, even if they're not exactly at the same place. Gently remind your kid that he or she has been through six boyfriends or girlfriends in the past year! Don't take a stand; make a suggestion. Remind him that college may be his last chance to play the field. Encourage her independence. Remind him of how much he hates being tied down. Be like the flowing stream that slowly dissolves away resistance, and not the sledgehammer breaking everything in its path. After all, the college years haven't even begun. You don't want to be completely alienated from each other before they start classes.

Decision Variables

After avoiding these potential problems, you need to help your child focus on making a sound decision. After your child narrows down his or her list of schools to a select few, it's time to get serious about items that make a difference. Those "personality inventory" tests that they can take as part of the recruiting process may be helpful. Some of these ask high school students to list the five most important things a college could offer. Others ask them to name five new activities they might want to try out in college, such as acting, singing, working on the yearbook, or learning a foreign language. The student then can seek a school that offers those possibilities.

Carefully questioning school officials may make the choice a little easier. For example, if your daughter says she has always wanted to try acting, call the theater department. In some larger schools with well-developed theater programs, only students who are drama majors are allowed to audition! If your youngster loves to be active in all kinds of activities, a smaller school may be a better choice.

Other items to think about, as mentioned earlier, include the size of the city, the location of the school and distance from home, the student-teacher ratio of the college, majors offered, campus activities, the school's prestige, and the general harmony between the school's "personality" and the student's temperament.

In some cases the actual choice of a favorite school is a no-brainer. Your kid may have known for several years which college interested her the most. Athletes have favorite coaches and teams that attract them to specific colleges. You can breather a little easier if this is the case, since there won't be much anxiety associated with actually making the decision.

Along this line, many schools offer what is known as an "Early Decision" day. The idea is to discover students who are willing to make an early and definitive statement that one specific school is their top choice. Often, high school seniors who are willing to make a strong commitment to one college receive what is almost preferential treatment in the selection process. In other words, the college admissions team may be willing to accept a student with less impressive credentials who submits an early application simply because the young person so strongly wants to attend the institution. Even when this is not the case, the early application option will place your son or daughter higher on the *waiting list* of those who wish to be admitted to a school, after the college has made its initial choices as to who may enroll. This strongly increases the odds that your child will be able to attend the place where he or she really wants to go, even if the school is a prestigious, selective institution such as Ivy League universities and other private schools with enrollment caps. Further, if your youngster is placed on a waiting list, he or she can take advantage of the time to apply to other schools that would be satisfactory, if the favorite doesn't come through. Early application decisions are normally announced in January, while regular admissions announcement dates usually are later—in March or April, or even after that.

The Waiting Is the Hardest Part

What parents need to understand about the enrollment process is that, at the same time the kids are making up their minds, the various schools are narrowing their lists down to the students who make the grade. Then the wait begins. Imagine what fun this brings. Each day your child goes through the mail and is disappointed when the letter isn't there. She agonizes every time there is no answer, or when the answer is "no." Naturally, he takes out the bad news on you. Brace yourself for a new level of angst and anger. After all, part of being a parent is being a punching bag.

One key date in your life, if it isn't already, is April 15. Not only is that day your tax deadline; many colleges have specified it as "Notification Day." They release lists of who gets in (and who doesn't) on that day. Talk about upping the ante! High anxiety is a major part of the application process, and revealing everyone's fate all at once makes the month of April particularly unbearable.

As a result, it's wise to try to help your youngster create diversions for the waiting period. They can:

- make up "backup" lists, in case their first few choices don't work out

- take up jogging and aerobics to run off some of the frustration
- swamp themselves in high school activities to help the time pass
- just be really hard to deal with—the preferred choice of most high school seniors

During this interval, these fine young people are also suffering from *senioritis*, a malady that grows to epic proportions during the second semester of the final year of high school. They don't want to be in school, and they're worried sick about the future. So they skip class, argue, pout, make bad grades, challenge authority, and treat you like dirt. This is all part of a divine plan. A great spiritual force has designed this time to make it easy for Mom and Dad to want their kids to get out of the house!

Finally, mercifully, a deal is struck. At long last the school and the student agree upon one another. Rejoice! Your child will receive an admissions letter stating that he or she can enroll. Some kids act real casual when this moment arrives. After all, exuberance isn't cool. Others slip—show some excitement and even smile at you! Either way, you should be thrilled, because this important moment reduces anxiety and tension for everyone. The sense of satisfaction may not last forever, and your child may, at some point, decide the selection was wrong. For now, though, you have survived a major chore in the college parenting process.

At the same time, you should be aware that, of every ten freshmen who start at a specific institution, as many as half will leave. Of those who quit, seven out of ten will re-enroll somewhere else, and many of those will graduate eventually. A college choice is not carved in stone. Leaving is not the same thing as failure; it's more like a change of address. Kids make mistakes when choosing their school. Still, these mistakes can be corrected. Starting at one place is only the beginning of the journey. The trip may take a long time and move along a twisted path.

How to Follow Up

Once the actual choice of a school is made, you should encourage your child to make a few visits to the campus, if at all possible. These trips serve several purposes. First, traveling gets him or her out of the house for a couple of days, giving you a much-needed break. Second, adjusting to the campus in September will be easier if the new student has learned his way around, even just vaguely, by exploring a few buildings and looking into open dorms. A little familiarity created in the summer will go a long way in the fall. Third, the on-site visit may help confirm that the choice was indeed a good one. It commits the youngster, who probably changes his mind every ten minutes, to the course of action. After all, you don't want to have to go through all this mess again. So, even if you have to donate a few dollars to the road-trip fund, extra pre-enrollment visits during the summer are a great idea.

Meanwhile, your son or daughter will be plotting and scheming. Just like a kid in a candy store, a new high school graduate thinks of all the things he can do with the newfound freedom that accompanies going away to school. Table 5.1 indicates a few of their intentions.

Table 5.1
What Will Change Once They Hit Campus

- hairstyle
- hair color
- grammar and syntax
- diet (especially amount of types of junk food consumed)
- favorite television programs (no more "kid stuff")
- amount of skin revealed on an everyday basis
- political views
- attitudes toward drinking and smoking
- assessments of what's cool
- level of tolerance to Mom and Dad's rules
- level of tolerance to Mom and Dad in general

In other words, you're in for some big-time adjustments. Just as a total transformation of personality which took place during puberty and the teenage years, a new version of your kid will emerge with the onset of college life. As a result, you may want to enjoy, as best you can, her company during the final few months at home. Shoot some video, take some pictures, and store everything possible in your memory banks. These days won't last forever.

To Have and to Hold

As noted earlier, finding a college is much like finding a spouse. If there is a courtship, there must also be a marriage, and, as with every other wedding, the brunt of the cost is borne by the parents. You'll have to pull out your checkbook to pay application fees, registration fees, and even dorm room deposits, months before school ever begins. Grit your teeth, pay the fees, and hope for the best.

Remember that there are people in the world who go to a restaurant, order dinner, and, upon being served, start looking around at other tables. The next thing they utter is, "Gee, I wish I would've ordered that." Some husbands and wives do the same thing with other choices. Your child may, for a thousand different reasons, eventually decide that his original selection of a college wasn't a good one, either as a result of something as simple as immaturity or something as complex as the cosmic forces that change a person's mind without leaving even a small clue as to why. Go with the flow. The goal is survival, not being right or winning the privilege of saying "I told you so." The college years will shape the future of your progeny. Be happy they've decided to continue their education. Even if they change schools, they're still working toward a brighter and better future. Things will, more often than not, work out.

6

The Move, Registration, and First-Day Jitters

The summer before a young person leaves for college is more than likely going to be the most trying of your career as a parent. After all, your daughter or son is not a juvenile anymore, so you have to give them free rein. Naturally, your kid takes advantage and overdoes it, big time. You become frustrated, exhausted, and exasperated. What a great time to think about packing up all their things and moving them to school!

For those of you who will have live-at-home students, the quest to find some middle ground of adult versus child will continue right on. You may need some Valium or Prozac to function effectively during this time.

In preparing for the move from home to dorm or apartment, the first thing you'll discover is that your definition of "necessity" is vastly different from theirs. Study Table 6.1 meticulously. It outlines many of the basic arguments you're destined to have.

Don't let chaos rule the day. Compromise. Pick the stuff you believe is absolutely essential and let them pack the rest. They'll be back home sooner than you think. At that point they'll get the other things they truly need, so why have an unnecessary confrontation?

TABLE 6.1
Packing for College

What You Think They Need	What They Think They Need
toothbrush/toothpaste	mouthwash (for emergencies)
sheets	Cliff's Notes
blankets	Frisbee
reading lamp	Lava (or other make-out lamp)
razor/shaving cream	scissors to trim new facial hair
pillows	teddy bear, ball glove, or other childhood relic
warm clothes	"cool" clothes
backpack	backpack (for onetime use)
pajamas	nightshirt/gym shorts
typewriter	laptop and laser printer, CD-ROM drive, and Internet access
notebook and typing paper	computer paper
bookshelf or bookends	posters of hunks/babes (Brad Pitt/ Pamela Lee) or of favorite movies
record player	CD player with headphones; portable CD player (for jogging)
cold tablets	No-Doz
family picture	picture of significant other
coffee pot	plenty of Mountain Dew, Jolt, or other high-caffeine drink
laundry bag	fishnet to hang brewskies out the window on cold nights
stationery to write home	telephone to call home (collect)
basketball/football/tennis racket	video-rental card
glasses/cups/dishes	binoculars with secret booze compartment
antiques/collectibles for decoration	empty wine bottles for decorations
Bible	contraceptive device
subscription to *Time* or *Newsweek*	subscription to *Playboy, Playgirl, Penthouse,* or *People*

Next, prepare to load up vehicles. A small U-Haul normally works best, since overloading is the most common moving problem. A couple of big cars may do the trick in certain cases. Expect a strange ride to the school. Your child will exhibit his or her own unique brand of nervous behavior. This can take the form of mindless babbling, overnonchalance, or bravado. Some young people will be quiet as mice. This change of address represents a considerable upheaval for them, so weirdness should be anticipated and ignored, except that you should try to be supportive. Talk about the times when you moved, or about similar experiences. Let them express their reservations.

Once you arrive on campus, the first thing you'll encounter is difficulty parking. Probably not one college or university in the United States has enough parking spaces, and those available couldn't be more inconvenient. It will seem as if the school has intentionally decided to make your life miserable by designing a cruel obstacle course. It will take a series of long trips with arms full of cumbersome items to finally get your kid situated.

Another thing you'll notice is how ancient all of the other parents look. Expect to stop at the next available mirror to carry out a self-inspection. Reassure yourself about your youthfulness. Tell yourself, "I don't look *anywhere near* that old!" Say it with gusto, so that eventually you will believe it. Moving in is a trying time, for you and for your new freshman.

Orientation

Many colleges have adopted the idea that a smooth transition into the first few days of college life makes the entire experience more palatable, for both parents and students. Some schools require freshmen to enroll in an actual orientation class, even giving them an hour or so of credit to keep them interested. In other institutions orientation is a one-day program focused on personal safety, parking, and other mundane matters.

Orientation for students routinely includes tours of the campus, the library, dorms, and the cafeteria, plus advisement about courses to take during the first semester. In addition, the program may cover social issues such as dating and other adjustments. Orientation is a system designed to integrate the student into the school with as little trauma as possible.

For parents, the school may offer a form of orientation during the moving-in period. This event serves as an indoctrination in the ways of the school. There are several key things to remember at this point:

1. See if you can get the school to send your child's first few sets of grades to *your home*. Reviewing grades is like looking at a car wreck or other disaster. You don't want to know, but you have to look.

2. Discourage your children from signing a "Right to Privacy" clause. If they do, you can't get access to any information about their college career, even things as simple as their grades!

3. Ask as many questions about scholarships, grants, and other financial issues as you can think of when the school's bursar or scholarship officer speaks. There are often funds and payment programs available that can reduce your out-of-pocket costs or make paying the bill a little easier.

Orientation is your last shot at getting helpful information from the administration. At this point they're still willing to act deferential and be congenial with you. Once they've got your kid signed up, the parent-college relationship is transformed, possibly in ways you won't appreciate (see chapter 10).

Registration: or, Trial by Bureaucracy

There is nothing so infuriating as standing in line for three hours, only to reach the front and be told, "You're in the wrong line." Registration is crafted carefully by university administrators to do just that. New students need to be resocialized. They must be made to feel that they are merely insignificant faces in the shuffling masses. Some take this lesson with humility. Others become angry. It makes no difference. They still have to wait.

Have you ever heard of *closed classes*? This feature of college life has been with us since the dawn of humankind, or at least since the dawn of college. No class ever has enough seats. This procedure keeps everyone from getting an approved schedule on the first try.

You think, "Oh, how inconvenient." Wrong message. These young people need to learn patience, perseverance, and problem-solving skills. What better place or method than to sprinkle a schedule with inaccessible classes?

It's not as if it's entirely the college's doing. Take a close look at what new students want in a class schedule:

- they want no classes before noon, because they want to get up no earlier than 11:00 A.M.
- they want no classes that end after 4:00 P.M., because no one can stay interested in a class that late in the day, especially on Thursday or Friday
- they want only Tuesday–Thursday classes, so they can work more, play more, have longer weekends, and sleep more
- they don't want Monday night classes, because Monday Night Football is on in the fall; in the spring, they may not want Monday night classes because they have to get up for school on Tuesday
- they don't want Tuesday night classes, because that's their weekly happy hour night (not having a class on Wednesday means they can sleep in)
- they don't want Wednesday night classes, because they have to get up on Thursday
- a Thursday night class is okay in the fall, since they'll stick around on the weekends for football games and such; in the spring, Thursday night classes are iffy, because they want to get away to the beach on Friday.

What this leaves them with is the desire to schedule all classes between noon and 3:00 on Tuesdays and Thursdays, with a night class on Thursday in the fall, and possibly Monday in the spring. And they're livid when the university won't accommodate them. Give them a Friday 2:00–5:00 P.M. science lab and you have grounds for bombing the Military Science Building (or Old Main, whichever is closer).

Consider registration from the university's point of view. Some poor sap has to convince your child that a course in Shakespearean Characters and Their Motives is a great way to meet the general education requirement in English literature!

When all is said and done, odds are that your son or daughter will get twelve hours (four courses) or so, consisting of one class they wanted, one they needed, and two that will at least move them along to the point where they can take something more meaningful in the spring. No one is happy, so everyone has to try to make a silk purse out of this particular sow's ear.

The First Day of Class

At long last, the turmoil of preparation subsides. The student must actually attend class. You won't be there, of course, but odds are the event will cross your mind during the day, probably more than once. A wellspring of emotions and memories surges up.

Chances are you'll recall your first day of college, if you went. Recollections of campus life, with its joys, obstacles, fears, and hopes fill your memory banks. It's an odd feeling, but warm nonetheless, full of hope that your child's experiences will be even better than yours.

It's possible that memories of his or her childhood will make you feel old, tired, and foresaken. How did the time pass so quickly? The days of youth are gone forever. Sadness and a sullen outlook rule the day. There is a certain finality to this milestone, which differs from events that occur every year, such as birthdays, anniversaries, and holidays. An era has ended. That can be depressing.

On the other hand, your heart could also be filled with joy, especially if you thought this youngster would never grow into college material. Many families will rejoice because their new college freshman is the first of a generation, or even the first ever in their family.

You will probably be alone as you encounter the first-day blues, jubilation, or blues combined with jubilation, whether you are at home or in the workplace. You'll want to talk about it to anyone who will listen. What you probably will get, however, is mild support diluted by a good dose of disinterest. After all, someone else's kid is doing something completely different, and you don't care what their youngster is doing, now do you? And so the day passes.

Here is a sampling of your passing thoughts:

1. I bet he's nervous. I sure hope he does okay.
2. Those professors really seemed to know their stuff.
3. I hope my daughter will have some good classmates to help with her homework.
4. I'll bet he will get all A's!

Conversely, here's what your kids are really thinking:

1. I haven't been this nervous since the day I cut class, cracked the headlight, and forgot to empty the ashtray in Dad's car.
2. Where did they find this dweeb professor?
3. Wow, check out the hunk in the fourth row!
4. I can get a C in this class, no problem.

Class Conduct

Most college freshmen arrive to class late, because they've lost their schedules, they can't find the building, or they stayed too long hanging out in the student union and didn't allow enough time for travel. Never fear. The odds are great that they'll still beat the professor to the room. Why? Because a substantial number of professors believe freshman courses are their most onerous duty. So they'll be in the hallway arguing with the dean, saying stuff like, "But I had to teach English 101 at 4:00 P.M. Monday, Wednesday, and Friday *last* semester!" These complaints usually fall on deaf ears, and a grumbling faculty member eventually will shuffle in.

Most professors are relatively sympathetic to the plight of new freshmen, which means they wouldn't be surprised by the details of Table 6.2. The majority will be understanding; others will plunge through the first day without ever looking up. You might want to share Table 6.2 with your youngster, so he or she can avoid some early difficulties.

TABLE 6.2
Little-Known Facts About the First Day of Class

- Seventeen percent of students forget their schedules and can be found wandering the hallways in search of their classroom. Ten percent will give up and go home.

- The average freshman will fall in love twice (per class) on the first day.
- In every section of more than twenty students, one or two are destined to ask a series of annoying, obvious, brown-nosing questions that will gain them lifelong enemies.

In any case, after a few uncomfortable moments when everyone checks out everyone else, class time begins. Shortly thereafter, the student body is sent *en masse* to the university bookstore.

Remember registration? The experience of waiting in the line and being disappointed is training that becomes invaluable in the bookstore. Endless hordes of peers are trying to find the cheaper, used copies of college texts. (In chapter 1 you were warned about the phone call you'll receive from your child telling you that he or she needs an additional $200 for books.) Another obstacle in the bookstore is the empty shelf. Freshman classes have book shortages, because professors inevitably underestimate class sizes or order books late, or because bookstores fail to update lists, or because some students buy texts early for classes they later find out are closed. So after milling around and searching for hours on end, your poor child discovers a new word: back-order. It sounds innocuous enough, but what it means is that she will be without a text for the first three weeks of school, which will cause her to fall far behind, right from the beginning! Frustration training is a key component of early freshman education, and this is just one more element in the process.

The dawn of the first day of class then gives way to the intense morning of regular college life. What quickly follows is known as *reality shock*. Your child realizes, Oh, rats, I really have to *be here*. I have to *do homework*, and *write papers*, and...*take tests!* Oh, no, I have to *work!* This sinking feeling of being trapped in unfamiliar circumstances causes a degree of feeling helpless that you never thought your child would admit. It shouldn't surprise a new college parent much to get an "I-wanna-come-home" phone call within the first few days and weeks of the new semester.

When this happens, you will be required to give a "hang-in-there" speech to your new freshman. Try to distract them by talking about local events, being sure to focus on things they hated, so they'll be reminded of how excited they were to get out of your one-horse town and into big-time college life. Talk about the county fair and things at church. Babble on about your neighbors and any other subject you know will bore them to tears.

It's also a good idea to throw around a few bromides about how everyone gets frustrated and how fear is a normal part of the transition into college life. If you perform this important parental counseling role effectively, in a nonjudgmental, reassuring manner, you might find a new ally in this former rival for possession of the remote control. Remember how sick you were of watching MTV and of saying "Turn it down!" Keep thinking to yourself, I *have* to keep him in school! This internal pep talk should give you the energy and emotional power to be the most sympathetic and understanding college parents of all time. And he'll never know your real motive.

Even the most competent and confident eighteen-year-olds are likely to fall prey to reality shock. They ordinarily choose to brave these feelings without showing them to others. You, as a parent, will probably recognize that they're acting a little strange in the first few phone calls or letters. One way to let them know you're in their corner is to simply tell them you know about reality shock, even if you call it by a different name. It's okay to say stuff like, "I'll bet it seems a little strange to you. It's a whole new world, isn't it?" Anything to nudge them into admitting they're a little nervous works well. Then it's easier to offer words of encouragement. Any top-ten list of life's greatest stressors includes changing jobs and moving. A new college freshman is doing both, so a little bucking up from home can't hurt.

Following the completion of the first four weeks of classes, give yourself a reward. Your child has overcome the early barriers, and has established some semblance of a daily routine. The attrition rate (students dropping out of school) lessens sharply from there until the end of the semester (when it will dramatically rise again). You can enjoy about three months of freedom and relative peace of mind. Savor the moment. Once again, you have survived—for the time being.

7

The Freshman Experience

The first year of college is logically the one most parents would expect to be troublesome for their children. More often than not, it is. The freshman experience is comparable to a roller-coaster ride. High highs and low lows punctuate this venture out into the big, bad world. Those new freshmen are going to need help—some from you, some from their friends, and some from the university. To make it through the first year of college is a major victory. In many ways, it's all downhill the rest of the way, for them and for you.

New college students often encounter a common set of emotions and incidents. Their reactions are likely to include wide-eyed confusion; feeling scared, dethroned, and lonely; having bouts of homesickness; and being swamped by schoolwork. Each of these responses deserves some attention. Parents who are aware of what freshmen are about to undergo are in better positions to try to help.

Wide-Eyed Confusion

Any new situation is confusing. The traditional high school graduate spent three or four years in the same building and with the same teachers, and hung out with a gang of well-established friends. Even the behaviors of their enemies were predictable. Generally, the routine was consistent and placid. Walking across the stage and receiving a diploma meant this comfort zone was lost forever. Although this may not have dawned on your child at graduation, starting college will make it very clear. For openers, consider the surprises that await freshmen in college, as listed in Table 7.1. These factors will confuse them greatly.

TABLE 7.1

What Freshmen Don't Expect About College

- the amount of homework
- professors who don't care whether their students show up for class or not
- a roommate (especially if it's a roommate from hell)
- others' lack of interest in who they are
- being anonymous, or being in a class with over a hundred students, which means they'll be known by number and not by their name
- the lack of logical room numbering in old college buildings, making it real easy to get lost or be late to class
- the tremendous number of inaccessible but hot-looking men and women on display the first week of school

---

Parents should tell their youngsters to expect to be confused. A new place and setting requires a major adjustment. Settling down will be easier if your daughter or son was able to visit the campus before the school year began (see chapter 5).

Still, no matter how much you try to prepare them, they're going to be baffled by much of what they see. They're going to call home and fish around for help. Once again, explain to them that confusion is normal. Reassure your new college student that it won't be long until a new routine will be in place and everything will seem fine. Then, tell him or her that adjusting to a new environment is good practice for later on. Most people move several times throughout their adult lives. Learning how to adapt to a new city and set of circumstances is a life skill that everyone needs, sooner or later.

Feeling Scared

Most kids won't own up to being fearful about this new world, but you can be sure they are. College is a fresh challenge. They have new competitors, and the tasks, while familiar, aren't exactly the same. College courses demand more intensity and attention. Young people, at this stage, often wonder if they're good enough to make the grade. Those who were used to being the top dog academically in high school discover numerous classmates who are just as smart. Average students become troubled and question their own abilities, which makes life difficult.

Universities do their part to help by offering tutors for various subjects. In addition, professors are required to hold *office hours,* which are specific times when they make themselves available to students. As a parent, make sure your child doesn't shy away from the instructor and fail to take advantage of these resources. Most professors at one time or another actually enjoyed interacting with kids. Some have lost the feeling, but most are going to give the benefit of the doubt to a student who seems to be trying his or her best to succeed. They won't have patience, though, with students who never show up for class, or the ones who give the impression that they couldn't care less about learning.

Talking to a professor can be intimidating to a new college student. After all, profs often are called "Doctor," "Mister," "Misses," or "Professor." These titles alone are enough to make some kids uneasy. Parents should point out how important it is to get past the fear and approach the instructor if help is needed. Encourage your child to get to know the professor, at least a little bit. Some interaction will reduce the nervousness associated with asking a faculty member for assistance.

Even so, a small degree of anxiety may be good for freshmen. It keeps them on edge. Fear may cause them to exert more effort. Just as stage fright heightens the performance of a musician or actor, apprehension about school can be channeled into better effort and higher grades for students. Don't worry too much about a little healthy trepidation. A certain amount may help them become more focused during the first few crucial months of their college careers.

Feeling Dethroned

Those of you who know something about child psychology are familiar with the concept of dethronement. It starts with the firstborn child, who has had the run of the house for a few years. This child is "king of the hill," right up until the time the second baby comes along. Suddenly all the attention shifts to the new little one. The firstborn is dethroned. He or she battles for attention by being extra good, being extra bad, or reverting to earlier stages of development, such as thumb-sucking and bed-wetting. Only the ultimate baby of the family, the last born, does not have to experience this form of dethronement.

There is a second type of dethronement. During the senior year of high school, your youngster is once again the king of the hill. He has the run of the building. High school seniors tend to pick on juniors, sophomores, and freshmen. They certainly do not walk in fear. Confidence, swaggering, and disdain for younger students are common.

Then comes college. Dethronement for a college newcomer means being lost in the crowd. He's a nobody. She's not noticed. It's not so much that they get picked on. Rather, they are ignored. This humbling episode in their lives can be helpful. After being broken down by these new circumstances, it will be time to start building things up once again. Still, at the time, it's one more adaptation that must be made in order to succeed in college.

Universities offer some help with dethronement by providing counseling, as well as extra activities and social events intended for incoming students. Still, school administrators do not hold the key to your child's making this transition successfully.

You can provide support as your son or daughter shifts from high school senior to college freshman. One simple method is to remind him of what a hero he is to younger brothers and sisters, or how admired she is by friends who did not attend college. You can strengthen a dwindling ego by pointing out all of the ways he or she still is at the top of the heap. College freshmen need to hear—through letters, calls, and personal contacts—expressions of pride in past achievements, combined with comments about how great they will do in the future.

For the most part, college students must tackle dethronement on their own. If they can't be king of the big hill, it's possible to start working on their own new hill. It's a matter of becoming more established on campus. A couple of A's on quizzes and tests can help restore their confidence. Joining clubs and assuming leadership roles in any setting will make them feel more in control of their new environment.

Dethronement isn't a bad thing. It happens over and over, throughout life. It's important for people to be knocked off their high horses every once in a while. For new college students, it's just their turn.

Feeling Lonely

Unless your youngster heads off to college with several close friends, he or she is going to be lonely during the first few months of college. Parents receive forlorn phone calls, and most freshmen travel home frequently if they can, seeking out old friends. To combat loneliness, college people in charge of student activities create social events especially for freshmen, such as dances and mixers of various sorts. Parents can't assist much on the loneliness front, except to encourage their kids to get involved.

The critical ingredient for a lonely college student is to have one friend. It's amazing how much a familiar face can help. One interesting phenomenon about college is that kids become fast friends with people they ignored in high school—and even with some former rivals—when faced with a cold impersonal university where they are unknowns. Just making one *new* friend can make all the difference.

Loneliness on campus tends to be cured by time. Over time, as students take more classes and meet more people, they make friends. Romance blooms early and often in college, which means the foresaken freshman soon is a happy boyfriend or girlfriend.

Long-term isolation is bad. If you suspect your child is having a tough time fitting in and making friends, expect the odds of dropping out to increase greatly. While you can't do a great deal to help, you can always hope.

Homesickness

People embrace security. Home is a secure place for most eighteen-year-olds. The first few weeks (especially weekends) of college are prime homesickness seasons. It's just like when they went to camp as kids. Suddenly Mom and Dad don't seem anywhere near as much like awful tyrants. Nothing is more appetizing than a home-cooked meal. Don't be surprised if homesickness continues to pop up through all four (or five) years of the college experience.

The craving to return to the familiar confines of home probably will be strongest when they're bored. Weekends with nothing to do arouse the feeling quickly. Consequently, kids may resort to phoning you, or actually coming back for a quick two-day visit. Think of these as a kind of methadone. Be cordial and accommodating. It won't be long until they have enough activities to keep them away from home. Eventually you will begin to wonder if they will ever come around again. Mild homesickness is no big deal. A major case, when they dwell on it so much that their grades suffer and your phone bill skyrockets, is what you should worry about. Pushing them out of the nest is one of your key duties as a parent. Sooner or later, they need to stand on their own.

Being Swamped

How much of a procrastinator is your child? If the answer is "big-time," that's how swamped he or she will be after the first six weeks of school. Being overwhelmed by more strenuous levels of study is a natural consequence of attending college. The main lessons parents can provide in dealing with this problem are organization and prioritization. Hopefully your new freshman has already learned something from your example, unless you, too, are a major procrastinator.

Help your youngster cope with the burden of college by showing him how making a list of daily activities and goals. This should help him organize both his thoughts and his efforts. Stress the importance of prioritizing. Remind your daughter that when she feels swamped, the first question to ask is, *"What is the most important thing I need to finish today?"*

Buy your new college student a desktop calendar. It may not be used at first, but over time the importance of scheduling will become evident. Make up some story about how you used to take your calendar with you and write down the date of every single exam and the due date of each term paper during the first week of school. Your kid will know you're exaggerating, but still should get the point.

Also, be calm when she phones and tells you she can't handle it all. Encourage her to try. Suggest that it's not critical to do every little thing, but rather just the big things. Tell him getting behind can be a great learning experience, especially if he figures out how to avoid doing it every semester.

This is an age in which feeling overwhelmed by a crushing number of tasks and duties is beginning to seem normal. College kids must train to handle this challenge. If you can teach yours just a little about time management and organizational skills, the college years may be much more pleasant for them and for you, and your youngster will be better prepared for the future.

Odds and Ends

Surviving the freshman year is an around-the-clock task. Both parents and students have much to gain from a successful beginning. As your freshmen go through the seasons of this first year in college, they will flounder around seeking patterns and habits that will add to their comfort levels.

At first, many take the traditional route, attending football games, college-sponsored dances and parties, plays, concerts, and other on-campus events. As they adjust to the new environment, they begin substituting more personalized activities for these generic pastimes. Students are more likely to venture into town, take road trips, and generate their own social lives as time in college passes. As parents, you should be able to perceive some of this social evolution when you visit them at the school. Careful monitoring of their contacts during home visits, vacations, phone calls, and letters (see chapter 14) confirms that they are adapting to college life. It's a great feeling to know your young adult can indeed deal effectively with new surroundings. Meanwhile, a couple of other things might occur.

The Freshman Experience

The first is known as the *Freshman 15*. New
routinely gain or lose about fifteen pounds during the .
who were slightly overweight tend to lose. The great m.
gain weight. Why? Because they eat too much junk food, a.   .ase
dorm food is pretty fattening. Besides, the freshman year oc. .rs at an
age when a person's body starts to fill out. Don't embarrass him or her
by making a big deal about the Freshman 15. Unless the change in
weight is extreme, you don't need to say anything.

The Freshman 15 means new costs. Why? Clothes. Expect them
to hit you up for money to buy new outfits of whatever sort.
Christmas may be a big-time expense for unprepared parents, who
will receive some major requests from their growing children.

The second change will be in their language. They'll quickly
become accustomed to using *colorful metaphors* and probably will
try out a few on you. Your reaction depends on how you feel about
slang and profanity and the disrespect using these terms implies.
Some parents are comfortable with this new level of familiarity from
their kids. Others feel the need to sternly remind them "who you're
talking to." Either way is okay. Just expect it to happen. Your
collegian may slip and mutter a few words you've never heard him or
her use before.

Third, some freshmen enter an era of budding political activism
shortly after reaching campus. It's a time to wear a beret and
participate in various and sundry kinds of protests. Your daughter
may suddenly become a vegetarian and act all kinds of disgusted
when you eat red meat. Your son could decide to devote his life to
saving the ozone. Dozens of causes beckon the entering freshman
class each year.

Don't get too upset if this happens. Perhaps you were at one time
an idealist and protestor yourself. These involvements indicate that
your child has a passion for *something*, which, for the most part, is a
good sign, especially in this generation of me-first thinkers and
general complacency among young people. Only if the cause totally
interferes with things like going to class and making good grades
should you be upset. Besides, even if you are upset, what good will it
do? The more you push them away from these involvements, the
more drawn to them they are likely to be.

Academics

Most freshmen hate the majority of their classes. Don't be surprised if this happens. First they are often taking general education courses (see chapter 12). Freshmen will feel frustrated because they can't take classes in their majors even when they already have one picked out! Expect them to be disgusted by what they consider to be busywork that doesn't apply to the real world (as if they actually know what they'll need in the "real world"). As parents, it's your job to inform them that general ed classes are building blocks. Point out how their grades in these classes affect their odds of getting admitted to a major. Prepare a good set of "you-need-to-tough-this-out" speeches regarding their schoolwork. Let your child know that delaying gratification is not the strong suit of people in their late teenage years. The old "this-too-will-pass" line is probably in order.

Parents of about-to-be college students should be advised that it's possible for some freshmen to obtain credits in general education classes *before* actually setting foot on campus. Many high schools offer methods by which entry-level college courses can be taken during the senior year of high school or in the summer before the first fall semester. If your youngster is especially ambitious or intelligent, this is a good starting point.

Also, a few students are able to "test out" of certain classes by taking what are sometimes called College Level Examination Program (CLEP) tests. These tests provide students the opportunity to prove that they already have mastered the content of a certain subject. Individuals who pass CLEP tests are given credit for specific courses. Normally CLEP tests are administered in subjects such as math, English, history, and science.

Parents should be aware of two factors concerning CLEP tests. First, school officials, money grungers that they are, will often require students to pay tuition for the course, even though they don't actually take it! Big shock there. Second, CLEP tests are not the same thing as placement scores on the ACT or SAT. The score your child receives in English or math on the SAT or ACT may be used to determine the need for remedial work, as well as placement of students in advanced classes. This is a separate process from CLEP tests.

Are CLEP tests a good idea? They are, for some. If you have a mature, intelligent, motivated youngster who will take advantage of testing out of some fundamental classes, he or she will be less bored during the freshman year and will gain a sense of accomplishment by working ahead. If your child is less mature, taking a few classes where he or she is overqualified may build some confidence and give the new student a chance to excel without overexerting during the first year. It's up to parents to know which route is best for their kids, and then to try to steer them along the correct path.

At all times, remember: Freshmen are wet behind the ears, wide-eyed, dethroned, and all shook up. They are going to do foolish things (see Table 7.2). Therefore, parents must be cool, calm, collected, and together. After all, parents will often be the ones who will get the call when the new student has done something very silly and is just becoming aware of how it looked to everyone else.

TABLE 7.2
Goofy Things Freshmen Do

(Making It Painfully Clear That They Are Freshman)

- lock themselves out of their dorm rooms.
- lose their class schedules and have no backup copies
- call a professor by his first name and receive a robust rejoinder in response
- actually feel excited about the football team's first win
- ask a senior out on a date and receive a robust rejoinder in response
- wear sunglasses in class, thinking they look cool
- wear a high school letter jacket to class, thinking they look cool
- ask questions in class, after it's clear the professor is done and wants to quit
- use other obvious high school brown-nosing tactics that annoy their peers

- drive twelve hours to their high school sweetheart's college the weekend before a major exam, get rejected, and then have to drive home
- get so drunk that they puke in public, relieve themselves in inappropriate places, and can't find their way home

---

In general, parents should try to help without micromanaging. They should support without overindulging. It's a balancing act. Most folks make their way, for better or worse, with only a few minor false steps along the way. At times you'll be annoyed when it seems like your youngsters are ignoring the obviously top-quality advice you give them ("study hard and you'll do better on a test," for example). Still, when the job is done, you'll feel a great sense of relief. Next year should be a little easier. Just remember, the major emotions nearly all parents of college freshmen can expect to endure may be summarized in three little words: worry, Worry, *Worry!*

8

Fraternities and Sororities

Most of you probably have seen the film *Animal House* at one time or another, and wondered if sorority or fraternity life is really like that. It may be worse. At least in *Animal House* the good guys finally win. To be fair, Greek living is probably like any other form of housing. It can be excellent or it can be a nightmare.

Just as with other aspects of college, there is a matching process that should take place. Some students readily adapt to residing with "brothers" or "sisters," making lifelong friends and creating unforgettable memories. Others become lost in a cloud of—well, you know, boozy haze. The kind of young person who tends to enjoy the Alpha Beta Theta system usually has these characteristics:

- is outgoing
- likes group activities
- doesn't mind sharing bathrooms
- enjoys projects and other organizational ventures
- knows how to cook
- doesn't mind practical jokes
- can endure a certain amount of being bossed around

In larger universities, fraternities and sororities often form based on something in common, such as a college major, athletics, and even race. Frequently a specific sorority is matched with a fraternity.

These couplings increase the odds that romances, both short-term and long-term, will develop. Jointly sponsored dances and other social events are designed to keep members in good company, so no one endures too many lonely weekends.

In other words, joining a frat house or a sorority may reduce the sense of isolation that often goes with the freshman experience (see chapter 7). Also, the tutoring and assistance given by older Greeks to younger members may help a youngster to be less confused, scared, or swamped by schoolwork. Fraternities and sororities do tend to help make the transition from high school to college go a little more smoothly.

As a parent, you must ask yourself if the Greek system is a good idea for your child. Bear in mind that you will not have any final say, but you can make suggestions. Some parents, who had great experiences while in college, want the same for their sons and daughters. This leads to *legacies,* or kids who join the same fraternity or sorority where their parents once lived.

Other parents have certain concerns about the environment in these residences. They worry about too many parties, too much alcohol, or too much snobbery. Many distractions are found in Greek houses. One good approach is to learn how the system works, then begin subtle navigation toward the position you believe is best.

Major Aspects of Greek Existence

Besides social activities, there are other pros and cons of fraternity and sorority life that parents should consider. One, naturally, is cost. Pledges pay membership fees and badge costs, donate funds for altruistic activities, and collectively share the expenses from parties and gatherings. Compared to dorm life and other residential arrangements, the cost of being in a fraternity or sorority may be substantially higher. Guess who your kid will go to for the additional money?

Then there is the nutritional aspect. If your child lives in a dorm, food service is ordinarily provided. This means he or she has a decent chance of eating at least one nutritious meal per day. Many fraternity and sorority houses have kitchens but no cooks. The upside of this arrangement is that your kid *might* learn how to prepare a meal. The downside is that he or she may simply eat junk food and avoid anything that's healthy.

Finally, there is the often-forgotten reason for all of this in the first place, which is *getting an education.* Many Greek houses require first-year members to attend study halls or other functions where they are forced to actually crack the books. These practices are most prominent in athletically oriented houses. Either way, it's one of the positive things the organization can offer its participants.

At the same time, parents should be aware of another side of Greek life that isn't so positive—in the area of academic integrity. Many houses maintain what are called *frat files,* which are collections of old tests accumulated over the years by previous students. These files allow Greeks the advantage of seeing old exams to which other students do not have access. To neutralize this practice, professors either must change their exam questions or test formats constantly, or simply provide copies of past tests to all of their students. Either way, studying a test is not the same as studying the actual material, and the student who cheats in this way hurts his or her own effort more than anyone else. You, as a parent, can let your son or daughter know that you are aware of frat files and discourage him or her from yielding to the temptation. Don't expect to have much influence relative to the peer pressure they will receive.

Worse, previously submitted term papers and other projects may also be kept on hand by fraternity and sorority leaders, allegedly as guides for pledges to follow. Professors know where this can lead—to *de facto* if not deliberate plagiarism. Again, faculty members try to change writing assignments sufficiently so that these "recycled" efforts will be noticed, but only professors who are aware of the practice can participate in policing the problem. As parents, it is worth telling your child that there is a real moral issue involved in plagiarism and that using someone else's work denies them a valuable part of their education. Writing skills are key components in successful careers in many occupations. Stolen papers mean a lost opportunity to practice writing effectively.

Parents realize that their moral training probably ended in the early teen years. You can only hope that your prior counsel (and more importantly, your example) will convince your son or daughter to take the high road in college life.

As important as these ethical issues are, there are also some practical concerns: Students who slide by using these tactics tend to make lousy employees in later life. They also will have received substantially less for their (your) educational dollar. The best you can do, however, is to simply repeat what you tried to teach in the past. This is a touchy subject, but one you should discuss with your new college student. Assure your child that an honestly achieved grade of B (or even F) is more satisfactory to you than an A garnered by cheating. College can be stressful. Deadlines come and go. The temptation to take the easy path is great, but the rewards of academic honesty are far greater in the long run.

Phase One: Rush Week

Fraternities and sororities, believe it or not, have a vested interest in attracting outstanding young people. Successful students keep house grade point averages (GPAs) up, which matters to the administrators who charter various groups. Talented athletes give the unit another form of prestige. Good-looking people are sought because they are thought to generate a positive image for the organization. Also, every house needs at least one comedian. As a result, Rush Week, or the week when new members are selected, is a major event for frat boys and sorority types, especially those in leadership positions.

One of the decisions faced by freshmen is whether or not to seek entry into one of the houses. If they decide to try, then they must decide which organization is the most desirable. For the uninitiated, the house's reputation is the major factor in the decision-making process. Several sets of forces will be at work as your youngster determines whether or not to apply. For one, there is fear of the unknown. After all, a major resettling has already taken place after arriving on campus and starting classes. Joining a frat or sorority and moving in would add one more layer. Second, apprehension about rejection may enter into the equation. Your son or daughter could be completely rejected by *all* of the houses, or merely not get into his or her first (or second, or third) choice. Being told you're not good enough hurts, especially during this time. Third, your child may have peers who roundly object to the whole Greek structure and who will make their feelings perfectly clear. Here are some examples of the kinds of things non-Greeks say about Greeks:

- "It must be awful to have to pay to have friends."
- "All they do is try to get someone from their house elected as homecoming king/queen."
- "You have to put up with all the crap, just so you'll have good business contacts after college."
- "Do you know what they do to pledges? I wouldn't let some senior tell me what to do all year."
- "They're a bunch of snooty socialites."
- "What a clique. They don't even speak to anybody but their own kind."

Clearly, in any discussion of the value of fraternity or sorority membership, differences of opinion will arise. If your offspring decides to join, he or she should go in with eyes wide open. The truth is, only a select group functions effectively in the Greek system. Others flounder. Your son or daughter should ask around, and get as much input as possible before seeking membership in one house or another. Having chosen this option, the next step will be to go to pledge parties.

During Rush Week, individual houses have gatherings where information is exchanged between the student and the organization. House recruiters tell freshmen about the house's history, activities, organizational structure, living arrangements, financial requirements, and pledge procedures. In return, the prospects supply information about their chosen majors, interests, past accomplishments, and so forth. Each side sizes up the other. Names, faces, and the distinctions between houses quickly begin to blur, as potential members are bombarded with possibilities. On the other hand, if your son or daughter is attracted by only one house, then he or she has "all of the eggs in one basket"—which can result in serious disappointment.

The Moment of Truth

At the close of Rush Week, leaders of the various groups gather and negotiate who gets whom. There is ordinarily quite a bit of wrangling for the high-status members (e.g., football stars, or 4.0 students). Those who are considered marginal prospects also receive careful scrutiny. No group wants to end up with someone who will be a continual source of misery. The in-between types fall into place relatively easily. Then the announcement is made, and each organization posts its list of new pledges.

At that point, you will probably get a ho-hum, exhilarated, or depressed phone call from your young college student. Those who got what they wanted will either be thrilled or not surprised. Those who didn't get into a particular house, or did not get in at all, will require some bolstering on your part. Refer to the list of things non-Greeks say about Greeks for ideas on how to address your youngster. Remember, however, there is a fine line between quality sarcasm and sour grapes. As you give solace, remind your son or daughter that every campus has a wide variety of academic and social organizations, each looking for involved members who will be welcomed with open arms. Greek life is only one option among many.

Pledging and Initiation

Old legends, and old habits, die hard. So it is with pledging ceremonies. You may have heard some of the horror stories about blood rituals, puke procedures, kidnapping and abandonment, and other drastic activities associated with Greek initiation rituals (especially in fraternities). Most schools have outlawed these practices, and most fraternity and sorority councils have endorsed the concept that there is a line between teasing and torture, embarrassment and harassment.

On the other hand, your son or daughter should expect to endure a certain amount of taunting, practical jokes, or silly tasks to perform. Most Greeks try to make the process more fun than humiliating. They still set up a pecking order, though, with new recruits at the bottom. This will require another emotional adjustment for your child, who is, after all, still establishing sea legs for college itself.

On a brighter note, he or she will probably create bonds with other newcomers to the system, and have a variety of fun parties and other social events to attend. Barbecues, dances, and many more festivities will quickly fill up the fall and spring social calendar.

Ordinarily some form of ceremony marks the conclusion of the pledging season. Soon after that the house settles into a routine that will continue on for the remainder of the school year. As a parent, do not become lulled into thinking this means all is well (or all is bad, for that matter). Table 8.1 provides a list of the things you might like or dislike about your child's life in the Greek house of his or her choice.

Body, Mind, and Spirit

College is designed to educate the whole person. Everyone tends to focus on the mind, but there is also the body and the spirit. Fraternities and sororities often fulfill bodily needs by creating opportunities to compete in all forms of intramurals, from flag (or powderpuff) football to basketball, golf, volleyball, tennis, softball, and others. Greeks also seem to be the ones who sponsor student Olympics of various types.

Given the pressure of college life created by exams, difficult peers, grumpy professors, term paper deadlines, and the never-ceasing search for companionship, it's good to have access to physical activities designed to relieve some of the tension. Young people should run, jump, collide, catch, and throw throughout their years in school. Fraternities and sororities are far above-average in encouraging these activities.

As for training of the spirit, well, don't expect much. Your youngster will probably learn more about consuming spirits than about things spiritual. Again, the values you modeled earlier in life are going to be the deciding factors as your child's young adulthood years unfold.

What to Do

It's difficult to know what kind of advice to give your freshman about becoming a frat rat or sorority sister. The list of pros and cons is long.

TABLE 8.1
The Greeks

Neat Things Greeks Do
- raise funds for local charities
- serve local volunteer organizations and outreach programs
- offer alcohol awareness programs for students
- develop study halls for new recruits; mentor and tutor members
- create networks during college and afterward, for both business and social activities
- provide opportunities to meet members of the opposite sex in places other than bars

Pathetic Things Greeks Do
- play loud music that annoys everyone in the neighborhood
- toss Frisbees or footballs, flexing and grunting, to try to impress the babes on game day
- pooh-pooh non-Greeks and dormies
- make cutting fashion comments about everyone except those in their own house
- do that phony hug-and-love stuff with each other when the homecoming queen is announced
- sing annoying Greek songs
- take over the best tables in the bar, harass the waitress, and fail to leave a tip
- stuff the ballot box in student government elections
- drink in large, obnoxious groups and make that "woooh" sound

What may be best is to just talk things over with your son or daughter and lay out the possibilities. This is one choice that might well be left for the young person to make. After all, if they hate being in the system, they can always quit.

Table 8.2 is a quiz you might want to give your kid concerning Greek life. Unfortunately, it would be difficult to get anyone to sit down and actually answer the questions. Instead, work them into the conversation at some point and carefully recall their answers. Then read chapter 9 to give yourself a fuller sense of how your child might find life in college to be. Also, feel a great sense of relief that you don't have to make the choice, realizing that you reside in a much more sane and stable home! And remember, odds are they'll be back to experience life with you early and often. Nothing lasts forever, especially in the cruel world of college housing.

TABLE 8.2
Questions Your Kids Should Ask Themselves
About Fraternity or Sorority Aspirations

- How many beers can I drink without showing the effects?
- How good am I at looking like I'm being friendly when I'm talking to someone I can't stand?
- Do I want to be part of the homecoming court?
- Do I really want to run for student government?
- Do I really want to be hooked up with these people, and this house, *for the rest of my life*?
- Can I study while my friends are playing *hall ball*, or some other loud indoor game?
- Do I have the self-discipline to study when everyone else is partying?
- When non-Greeks sneer, what will I say to them?
- Do I have the build for this?

9

Dorm Life and
Off-Campus Housing

Most people spend far too much time worrying about what others think. Their greatest fear is to be categorized as a freak or a geek. They're terrified others won't consider them to be hip or cool enough to be part of the in crowd. If worries about being uncool affect even middle-aged people, ponder the extent to which this issue may haunt your new freshman. To some new college students, especially those at larger, well-established campuses that have thriving fraternity and sorority systems, dorm life represents the epitome of potential geekness. Yet the daunting possibility exists that your youngster will live in a dormitory.

At many schools dorm life is the norm. Smaller schools and formerly single-gender campuses may have small or weakly developed Greek systems. In any case, whatever the reason, a large percentage of college students live in some kind of dorm arrangement. As a parent, it's your job to make certain your child does not feel like some kind of second-class citizen for taking this route. For youngsters with healthy egos, what others think about their living arrangements won't be a problem. Unfortunately, others may look wistfully and with envy at those who live in Greek housing or off campus. Either way, one thing is inevitable: Dormies encounter taunting. Here are some examples of the things Greeks say about non-Greeks:

- "What a bunch of dweebs."
- "What a bunch of geeks."
- "What a collection of dorks."
- "What a bunch of..." (you get the idea).
- "I'd hate sharing bathrooms like that."
- "Their dorm isn't even coed."
- "It must suck to have to sign in and sign out."
- "You can end up with an unbearable roommate, real easy."
- "Your intramural team stinks!"
- "Which dorm do you come from? Loser Hall?"
- "Eating in the cafeteria is like going back to high school."

The one great eternal truth about life in the United States is that young people seem to have a great need to deride their peers. Hostility between Greeks and dormies goes back to time immemorial. In any case, there are things you as a parent should know about the dormitory experience.

Roommates

After registering to live in a dorm, your son or daughter probably will be assigned a roommate. In some schools, the pairing is a matter of chance or random luck. In others, the college staff seeks to match roommates based on similar interests or backgrounds. There is, of course, no way to predict whether or not the two will be compatible. Many pairings which seemed like potentially great duos turn into disasters, and relatively quickly. Factors that can create these problems include:

- different sleeping habits (late-nighters versus early risers)
- drinking patterns and throwing-up schedules
- study habits, or the lack thereof
- arguments about who gets the room (when one has a boyfriend or a girlfriend and the other doesn't)

- contrasting personalities (for example, shy versus outgoing)
- musical tastes
- interpersonal "chemistry"

If your child continually reports roommate problems in the first semester of school, take them seriously. There is nothing worse than being miserable in your "home." An unhappy dorm life can be a major contributor to lower grades, the desire to drop out of school, and other difficulties. When an incompatible roommate is the issue, encourage your youngster to move on to a new setting. Normally this process works itself out, as students make friends and discover better potential roomies. If yours doesn't, be sure you and your youngster are proactive in finding more suitable living arrangements.

Be advised of one common fallacy: Having your kid simply move in with an old high school chum is not always the answer. Young people change a great deal as they migrate from high school to college. Often this results in the breakdown of old friendships, as new ones evolve. When high school pals think their friendships will remain unaffected by college, disenchantment often follows. It if does, your job as parent is to explain that such changes are a normal part of growing up. Your kid won't listen, but share these pearls of wisdom anyway, so they can be appreciated later in life.

In some circumstances, school officials will allow your youngster to live alone in a dorm room. This is an ideal solution if your child is:

- a loner
- sloppy
- fastidious and intolerant of those who are sloppy
- a light sleeper

It is best to find out in advance if the college offers single dormitory rooms. If it does not, and your kid simply can't tolerate the idea of a roommate, you may wish to consider off-campus housing (see the end of this chapter). If the school can accommodate individuals living alone, put in your request early. Many times single dorm rooms are considered to be luxury housing.

Coed Dorms

Another of your fears may be coed dorm arrangments, where young people of both genders live in the same building. Images of rampant towel-modeling, hallway exhibitionism, and promiscuity surely will enter your mind as you consider this prospect. The reality is, people between the ages of eighteen and twenty-five can and will find places to have sex, with or without coed dorms. Do both-gender dorms make it easier? Probably. Still, you have to consider a few things:

- What were *you* like at that age?
- Have you talked with your youngster enough so that he or she will at least use protection to avoid disease and pregnancy?
- If you advised that abstinence is best, this message either sunk in, or didn't, long before your child headed off to college.

Coed dorms offer certain advantages. For one, young men are more likely to behave in a civilized (or less uncivilized) way, which means the building is likely to be quieter. Outlandish and rowdy behaviors, which make for legends in male-only dorms, may be viewed as simply immature and boorish by the females who witness them. The net effect may be to limit unnecessary yelling and strutting throughout the course of the year. Some young men may even occasionally make their beds and change their sheets in case an innocent female wanders by and looks into the room.

Male-female partnerships for studying may also evolve in coed dorms. In general, studying is encouraged in these settings. It may be easier for either gender to seek academic help when someone from the opposite sex is there to lend a hand. In addition, young men and women may get to know each other in a different way, where sexual attraction becomes less of an issue and real friendships based on other types of compatibility can form. Some students may actually resist sexual temptation, knowing that a messy breakup following a relationship, no matter how brief, may make home life uncomfortable.

Coed dorms normally have some kind of council, or leadership group, which is elected to help set building policies. These teams give your child a chance to assume a leadership role in a unique setting. They also teach males and females to cooperate and work together to resolve issues and problems. At a basic level, any form of group or team skills that evolves out of coed living will serve your college student well as a practicing adult.

Some coed dorms are arranged by floor, (male-female-male) while in others young people of both genders are assigned to rooms on the same floor. The primary concern for these men and women is bathroom access with privacy, which is a continuing issue through the years, especially during marriage. Thus, the coed experience may be an even more valuable form of later-life training.

Remember that privacy in general is something that becomes compromised in a dorm. At best your youngster can close the door, which is hardly the same as shutting out the world. This form of communal living, whether coed or not, is often a major and difficult adjustment for an eighteen-year-old, who just a few months previously felt as if he or she was the center of the universe. Even showering alone becomes an indulgence of epic proportions.

What They Should Expect

The vast majority of dorm arrangements in the United States include meal services. As a result, the *potential* exists for your youngster to eat three square meals a day. Don't count on it. If your kid grew up on a farm, you can be confident that your collegian will get breakfast, and a hearty one at that. In addition, he won't have to stand in line to eat, since no one else gets up at that time of day (unless, of course, your child is on an ag campus—then there will be a major traffic jam at the meal trough at 6:00 A.M.).

If your kid grew up in the city, rest assured that your son or daughter will have access to a healthy, though bland, lunch and dinner menu. It is absolutely amazing what dorm food services can do with cheese, bread, hamburger, and tomato paste. Many of the current food providers also set up ice cream machines, salad bars, and other incentives for your kid to eat right—or at least eat. Milk, chocolate milk, soda pop, tea, coffee, and some odd-looking red and yellow "fruit" drinks will be available at every meal. Your biggest frustration with the food service company may be that you're paying for three meals a day, seven days per week, but your kid eats there only half of the time. Don't despair, however, because even then, the cost is fairly reasonable. Food services count on no-shows when they set fees.

Another item that will probably cause your offspring to complain about dorm life will be the sign-in/sign-out desk at the front door. Most dorm managers want to be able to account for the whereabouts of residents and nonresidents, especially after 1:00 or 2:00 A.M. It's not that they don't trust your child; it's that they don't trust anyone. Be thankful this level of security exists. Campus leaders have become increasingly aware of the need for escort services, on-campus police phones, and other precautions to protect all students. Your youngster may gripe, but make it known that you think sign-in desks are a great idea.

A major factor facing college kids who live in dorms is socialization. Like people in most settings, they will tend to make friends with and hang out with people who are in close proximity. As a result, each dorm floor tends to take on an identity, evolving over time, and become known as:

- the study floor (lots of studious types)
- the party floor
- the hunk floor
- the babe floor
- the jock floor
- and, yes, the geek floor

Don't despair if your youngster ends up on the geek floor. Your kid may feel like a member of that sorry group from the film *Revenge of the Nerds*. Remind them of this: What is routinely ignored is that at the end of the movie, the nerd gets the girl and those beasties, the frat rats, just get theirs. It's no coincidence that the nerds of college life become leaders, inventors, and *rich folks* in the years to come. (For instance, what do you see when you look at Bill Gates?) Smarts and computer skills may not get you invited to the dance, but they do open a few other doors in the workaday world. You and your young college student should take some comfort from that.

Numerous other identities—some of them based on a single legendary incident—may emerge. Small-college dorm floors and even some dorm floors in larger schools may actually "will" the floor nickname from one generation of students to the next, which gives the place a sense of continuity over time. There may also be some legends perpetuated about key personalities who lived on the floor in the past.

For you anthropologists in the audience, watching legends and stories grow as they are transmitted through the culture of a geographic region (no matter how small) is not new. You know that a sense of identity, even if it's just affiliation with a dorm floor, may be an important ingredient in the well-being of someone who might otherwise feel lost in an ocean of nonentity. Suffice it to say that having a sense of belonging is normally a pretty good deal for your kid. It's probably wise to resist the temptation to denigrate your kid's dorm floor identity with words like "cute" or "silly" or "ridiculous." Let your kid have a little fun with this aspect of life within the peer group.

With regard to culture, another potential advantage exists in the dormitory. Foreign students often choose or are required to live in college-sponsored housing. So what, you ask. Remember, one of the key goals of a college education is to *broaden the horizons* of the next generation. What better way then to gradually and naturally expose them to other cultures and religions? Young people tend to make friends fairly easily, which means that, if adults will just stay out of the way, your son or daughter could emerge from the university experience with a deeper, broader understanding of the world. Not only that, a new kind of understanding and respect can develop from interacting with students from other countries. As a parent, who could ask for more?

Dorm life can be a learning experience or a travesty. Table 9.1 lists some of the things a student might like or hate about dorm life.

One variation of dorm life is housing units for married students. Some young couples find these miniature apartments a great way to make ends meet while finishing school. If your son or daughter is married and is tempted to drop out of school and seek quick money in the labor market, make sure you let him or her know about married housing. It may be the difference between a career at K Mart and a career on Wall Street.

TABLE 9.1

The Pros and Cons of Dorm Life

Good Things About Dorms

- food without cooking
- access to the campus, which is normally within walking distance
- intramural teams
- laundry facilities (for emergencies when they don't have time to bring their dirty clothes home to you)

Crummy Things About Dorms

- water balloons from the top floor
- noise
- community bathrooms and showers
- at least one obnoxious idiot on each floor
- it's hard to sneak in a keg

Off-Campus Housing

If you search the deep recesses of your mind, you may recall a time when just having your own apartment seemed like the ultimate in opulent and extravagant living. Expect the same from your own children. To many eighteen- to twenty-year-olds, the allure of living independently is almost overwhelming. As a result, it shouldn't surprise you if your new freshman or graduating high school senior expresses the desire to live with a few friends in an apartment or rental house while in school.

Some colleges, especially smaller private institutions, have policies requiring students to live on campus, at least for the first year, unless they continue living at home. In those circumstances, you won't even have to discuss the possibility of off-campus housing right away. (One reason schools insist on keeping students on site is largely financial; full dorms are needed to keep the proper cash flow. Also, some administrators think students don't get the full college experience unless they live on campus.)

If a student has several options—fraternity or sorority, dormitory, or apartment house—there are a variety of concerns you will need to address. For starters, there is the issue of maturity. Only those with sufficient willpower to get out of bed and go to class in the morning should consider off-campus housing. There are many temptations that could keep them home. Living off campus means there will be more demands on their time, including the necessity of working, at least part-time, in addition to doing their cooking, cleaning, bill-paying, and other tasks that accompany this form of autonomy.

Roommate problems in apartment settings are legendary. Two or more people have to learn how to divide chores, split the bills, and share space (not to mention showers and bathrooms). Noise levels, entertainment arrangements, and numerous other disputable items must be resolved if collegiate apartment dwellers are going to get along. Sharing a house with other students is almost like being married, in terms of responsibilities, but without some of the incidental benefits of matrimony.

Costs are a key factor. Besides rent and food, there may be additional expenses such as utilities and car expenses. Off-campus residents will probably need more furniture (even if it's just empty milk crates for tables) and other household support goods. You can expect them to "borrow" more of your things, probably without asking first, and to need more cash for incidentals. A person who will do well living off campus probably has to be:

- organized
- responsible
- cost-conscious
- tolerant (if with a roomie)
- willing to work
- craves freedom more than convenience

Talk to your youngster thoughtfully about the off-campus option.

Living alone at that age is not for everyone. It's easier to get lost and lonely off campus. Off-campus housing may mean missing out on some of the fun and frivolity that goes with being at school all the time.

Young people attracted to life off campus tend to be either serious-and-independent types, or overly gregarious. Probably you know which group includes your youngster. Serious students often fare well off campus, whereas budding socialites might be better off living where the structure of dorm life, or even fraternities or sororities, may cause them to focus more often on schoolwork.

Remember, the decision to move off campus is not carved in granite. If things don't work out, your college student usually can return to campus. Whatever happens, the experience of living off campus is another step toward leaving the nest finally and fully. Take pride in your child's impulse to launch out on his or her own. On the other hand, be aware that your son is probably saying to his friends something like, "Be it ever so humble, there's no place like your own babe lair."

Alternative Housing, On-and-Off Campus

Many university communities also have varying forms of special interest housing. The commune of the 1960s has given way to arrangements such as the Malcolm X House, Vegetarian House, French House, German House, Women's Studies House, and numerous other non-Greek and non-dorm coed homes. These units offer a wide variety of payment programs, such as working in exchange for lodging, or sharing costs. In addition, eating patterns, sleeping arrangements, and political activism programs are part of the house's method of operation.

Some students find these alternatives highly attractive. They are a great way to make a political statement, to annoy parents, and to meet other unique and passionate individuals. Some moms and dads become quite suspicious and sound real pious when they talk about these houses, which is probably a mistake. A better approach is to think of these living arrangements as a get-it-out-of-your-system plan. After all, the flower children of the sixties are now the parents of kids in college and should hardly cast the first stone regarding social consciousness, no matter how it gets expressed. Besides, as is true for other forms of college living, if it doesn't work out, your son or daughter can always move!

The Worst-Case Scenario

For many, if not most, parents the worst-case scenario may very well be to have your child live at home while in college. Probably the single biggest factor in such an arrangement is cost. Kids live at home to save money. Theirs, not yours. They expect you to pay for food, insurance, gas, and who knows what else. Also, they end up challenging you on every front, having concluded that they are now adults and should be treated accordingly. In short, *they will want to renegotiate every aspect of your home life*, including:

- when they sleep and when they're awake
- curfews versus coming and going as they please
- discipline or sanctions for inappropriate behaviors
- who pays for what (allowances?)
- what kind of language they use
- dress codes (and the lack thereof)
- hairstyles
- their right to pierce body parts, have tattoos, or indulge in any other form of self-mutilation currently in vogue
- car privileges
- their inalienable right to stay in the shower long enough to use up a week's supply of hot water
- smoking rights
- drinking rights
- bed-making requirements
- phone usage and long distance calls to long-lost boyfriends or girlfriends
- the right to show up for meals at their own convenience, and, of course, unannounced

In short, do yourself a favor. As soon as you can, push them out of the nest. You may believe it's costing you less to keep them home than it would to pay for them to stay elsewhere, but there are other intangible costs. Getting your kids out of the house is your only chance to retain a semblance of your youthful appearance and a positive outlook on life. You're not a lion. You can't just eat your young. Work it out some other way.

10

When the Bill Arrives

You were warned. Oh, yes, you were—back in chapter 1—about the costs of college. There is no avoiding the sense of sticker shock that accompanies your first *Tuition and Fees Statement* when it arrives in the mail, even when you think you're completely prepared. Expect to feel angry, betrayed, frightened, and bewildered all at once. These emotions run deep and they run wide. As a result, it's probably best to deal with each one individually.

Anger. Simply put, *they don't tell you* about all the things they consider to be normal college expenses when they recruit you and your kid. If they did, you probably wouldn't let your youngster enroll in the first place! Table 10.1 is a sampling of the fees you knew nothing about. Some or more of them will definitely make you angry.

Now, if this doesn't make you angry, run for Pope, because you have the patience of a saint! Most normal folks just want to pick up the phone and unload on somebody.

Betrayal. You trusted these people. You trusted them with the well-being of your most treasured gift—your child. What did they do in return? They relieved you of your second most treasured gift—your savings account! First there was all that warm and fuzzy stuff when you visited during the recruiting season, and then they

TABLE 10.1
Typical College Fees

- matriculation fee (cost of saying "yes, I want to go here")
- incidental fees (student government, entertainment, etc.)
- health care fees
- parking fees
- fee for taking fewer hours than they define as a "normal" course load
- fee for taking more hours than they define as a "normal" course load
- lab fees
- dorm charges
- extra fee for a single room in a dorm
- food charges for dorms
- refrigerator rental for dorm room
- telephone hookup
- extra telephone line for computer/fax/Internet
- general-purpose surcharge
- late fee for paying bill late (and they make sure you pay it late)
- interest on unpaid balance
- fee just because they can charge a fee
- library fee
- late-book library fee
- interlibrary-loan fee
- sports event ticket prices
- parking ticket fine (and they make sure everyone gets a parking ticket the first week of school)
- extra fine for paying parking ticket late
- add/drop fee for changing classes
- late fee for adding/dropping/changing classes after a ridiculously early-in-the-semester date

- fee deducted from tuition refund for classes dropped during the semester (the school keeps about 25 percent of the tuition paid for any course your kid dropped!)

and finaly

- a graduation fee, because they know they can zing you one more time!

---

hugged and loved you some more during moving-in or orientation week. *Now they've got you, and they know it.* They know that you as parents have finally adjusted to the peace and quiet of a less crowded nest. They know your hopes and dreams depend on your child's educational growth. You don't want the kid back, not just now. So you'll have to pay their exorbitant fees, just to maintain the status quo at home. What a system—robbery without a gun! Consequently, it's easy to feel betrayed, especially by that little snot-nosed recruiter who convinced your child to attend this college, and by that financial aid officer who said everything would be just fine. If you could just get your hands on them now, well, you'd be wringing their necks!

Fright. "How am I going to pay for this!" you ask, in terror. "Will he think I'm an inadequate parent if I say I can't afford it?" (The answer is, "Of course he will!") "What am I going to do?" This goes on for *four years!*

First, take a deep breath. Next, think as calmly and as rationally as possible about all the payment options presented in chapter 2. Hopefully you signed up for at least one of them!

No matter what payment options you choose, unexpected expenses are always frightening and frustrating. At your age—and like it or not, you aren't getting any younger—debt is especially troublesome. Besides, these obligations may mean you have to cut back on your lifestyle. What kid is worth that? Well, yours probably is, and so, like most parents before you, you'll no doubt be willing to make some sacrifices for a few years while your kid lives the life of Reilly.

Bewilderment. Look closely at the tuition statement. Most plans to eliminate the national debt are less complicated than this form. It's designed to be that way. Schools figure that by using smoke and mirrors they can get your money and make everything appear to be deceptively official, all at once. You will venture into the wonderful world of debits and credits, though the college will undoubtedly use them backward from everything you learned twenty-five years ago, in Accounting 101. There will be add-back fees, uneven balances, columns that don't add up, subnotes, smudges, and who knows what else. There will be, however, one crystal-clear part that reads: **Amount Due: Pay now or the student will be dropped from school** (Visa and MasterCard accepted). Expect your blood pressure to rise when you see those words.

A few parents make the mistake of calling the administration for an explanation. Bad idea. The phone will be answered by an overbearing, know-it-all clerk who really knows nothing except how to say, "It's university policy." The clerk can't decipher the bill either, so his best approach is to act as if *parents* are the ignorant ones. The temptation to yell, scream, and curse this imbecile will mushroom, right up until the moment when you remember:

- "This clown could mess up this and every other bill, for the *next four years!*"
- "This jerk could get my child thrown out of classes for late payments."
- "This moron could hold back my kid's grades, claiming nonpayment of tuition."
- "This °%#&@ might even stop transcripts from being sent out after graduation, meaning my new college graduate will move home when he can't get a job!"

It's worth repeating: *They've got you, big time, and they know it.* This makes it necessary for you to act deferential and placate some joker most employers would fire in a minute. Don't expect any help. Just break out the checkbook, bite the bullet, and pay up.

If you have a friend who is an accountant, have him or her help you understand the charges, and how the billing department credits your account. The primary thing to check for on the statement is evidence that you received any fee reductions you were entitled to, such as scholarships, special abilities grants, and other funds. Make sure they have in fact been deducted from your bill. Student account offices do make mistakes. You'll have to be a tiger to get them to admit it, and success only comes if you hang in there tenaciously until the statement is eventually corrected. Against your instincts, try to be as polite as possible with them, no matter how incompetent, stubborn, or uncaring they are. Expect to encounter a whole series of loops in their voice-mail runaround system. Keep asking to speak to someone higher up, and sooner or later you'll find someone who may actually know what he or she is doing.

It's Not Just the College You're Mad At

The trauma associated with receiving your child's first tuition bill probably has more than one cause. What you've read about so far is the sense of anger, betrayal, fright, and bewilderment directed at university personnel. There are other individuals who may be the focus of your wrath. Most notably, there is a sense of frustration that may be directed toward your kid. Probably the biggest question you're asking yourself is *"Am I getting my money's worth?"*

Remember, by now you're likely to have received your son's first *down slip,* which is a note from the college saying he is earning a grade of D or F in one or more of his classes. Perhaps your daughter has been telling you she's broke and needs more spending money. It makes you wonder if they're really trying, or if you're just throwing money down some kind of collegiate rat hole. As a result, some hostility may spill over toward your freshman. He or she may be surprised, when you call or visit, that your tone is pretty hostile. Why would you be so upset? So, before you blast your youngster, think about who and what you're really mad about.

The best way to manage your feelings about money is to consider college funding as an investment rather than a cost. If you put up some dollars now, it's possible your kid won't need to ask for as many dollars later (and you'll be in a better bargaining position if he asks anyway). In turn, he or she is forsaking some independence now for an even greater sense of freedom and opportunity in the near future. It's a trade, really, not an expense. Probably the three biggest questions that should be asked about money are:

- What do they need?
- What do they want?

- How much do we have to pay?

What They Need. Be aware of the differences between what students think they need and what you think yours needs. If you've forgotten already, refer back to Table 6.1 in chapter 6. Besides packing-for-school supplies, there are many other potential differences of opinion that may arise over necessities. For example, you believe what they need boils down to:

- tuition and books
- room and board
- a minimal amount of money for gas/spending money

What *they* think they need includes:

- date money
- spring-break slush fund
- road-trip expense account
- booze and/or cigarette budget
- newest hot CD allocation
- concert ticket allotment
- video game miscellaneous expenses
- long-distance telephone support
- munchies money

This is just the beginning. Some kids can only live in the newest designer clothes. Others can't breathe without redoing their hairstyles on a regular basis. Many won't be seen in public without a set of hot wheels. These sundries, you would argue, are *what they want* rather than what they need. Don't kid yourself. At their age, they make no distinction between the two.

How much? This is a major issue, since the first question you want to ask is, "How much should they contribute to their own education?" No one can answer that for you, since family incomes vary so greatly. Some reliable, strong-willed individuals will *insist* on paying their entire way. Others are equally insistent that their money is *their money,* meaning none will go toward the actual educational costs, which Mom and Dad are expected to pay. Unfortunately, this leaves you in the difficult position of bargaining with an eighteen-year-old, which is a major bummer.

At the same time, it's critical to remember that any transaction can be renegotiated. If your son or daughter is not holding up their part of the bargain by going to class and getting decent grades, negotiate! If he or she seems to drive newer cars, wear nicer clothes, and eat at better restaurants than you do, bargain!

Probably the biggest issue arises when you believe that your youngster isn't trying hard enough or doesn't appreciate what you're doing. When Mom and Dad conduct a cost-benefit analysis regarding the dollars they're putting out and see their kid making a half-hearted effort, the potential for real conflict quickly blossoms. College professors will tell you that, more often than not, it's the young traditionally aged students who are the most prone to taking school for granted and not giving much of an effort as a result. So, if your kid eventually flunks out or leaves school because of a failure to apply sufficient effort, he or she may eventually return as an older, nontraditional student and then get the most out of college. Not only that, but the final "I told you so" will belong to you!

Some kids resent the fact that their parents didn't send them to a high-prestige, high-priced institution. Feeling slighted and short-changed by this, they either goof off most of the time or constantly complain about having to settle for a low-caliber college. If you hear such a complaint, remind them of this: College is like everything else in life—you get out of it what you put into it. There are many dog-and-pony-show speakers running around the country, telling their audiences that they can obtain a Harvard-like education anywhere. After all, schools like Harvard use many of the same textbooks, videos, lab equipment, and case-analysis techniques found at practically every major university. The secrets to getting an education are effort, intensity, attention, and attendance! You don't *owe* your kid *any* college. You're giving a gift to him or her by helping with educational expenses. Don't let your kid tell you anything else. Point out to this ingrate that a diploma from a prestigious school such as Yale, Dartmouth, or Lehigh does one thing really well: It helps new graduates get interviews for good jobs with good companies. After that, however, a diploma and a quarter will buy them a phone call. Once a career is underway, it's performance—not pedigree—that leads to success, promotion, and all that other Great-American-Dream stuff.

If your college student keeps slacking off, and continually talks about how much she resents your meddling in her life, cut her loose! There is a big, bad world out there, and she will find it only too soon. If she needs to be shoved in that direction a little earlier, so be it.

Speaking of the outside world, there is one time and place where work beyond the classroom can become an active and integral part of a student's education. It's called an *internship program*. These programs allow students to work in actual businesses or in various organizations such as legal aid offices or governmental agencies.

If your child's college does not offer internships, contact school officials and talk to them about starting such a program as soon as possible. In practically every major, something is to be gained by getting hands-on experience before graduation. Some will learn they've chosen the wrong major (see chapter 12). Others will benefit from the opportunity to see theory and practice woven together for the first time. For a few, an internship may be the closest thing to an actual job they've ever had, and the difference between taking classes and being employed will become quite evident quickly.

Students of business, technology, journalism, science, and anyone else who can try out a career before embarking on it will be better off. You wouldn't buy a car without kicking the tires and taking a test drive. Most people don't marry without dating first. The kind of commitment required to obtain a college degree means that the school should accept its responsibility by making certain the new graduate will actually enjoy his or her upcoming career. We already have enough insurance agents who used to be English majors!

Overcoming Your Emotions

College costs can create some serious baggage—in many forms. Parents often resent having to lay out a lot of money, especially if their youngster's last few years at home have been tumultuous. Sufficient time may not have passed for old animosities to mellow and for peace to develop. When your new collegian seems ungrateful, unhelpful, or uncomunicative, the anger, fright, betrayal, and bewilderment that accompany large, unexpected bills will indeed extend not only to the university but also to your kid.

Talk to your daughter or son. Explain that you want to help without feeling used. Believe it or not, most young people don't like being dependent. Having to relinquish control over their choices may be part of the emotional baggage they're carrying around. College is a time when teenagers want to establish themselves as young adults. That's tough when they're also standing with hands open, asking for assistance. Use the issue to help establish a stronger, more mature relationship with your child. Reassure her that you don't mind the expense—in fact that you are happy to be paying it, because it means you're providing the final important cornerstone for her future, and that you simply want to make sure she is holding up her end of the bargain. Tell him you have every intention of getting even, by becoming a major burden to him in your old age, and that these dollars are a small investment in the significant expenses he will incur later in life, taking care of you!

The Conflict You Don't Want

By now it should be clear that college finances can create a battleground. Skirmishes break out between you and the university. Dissension can arise between father and son, mother and daughter. The war to be most carefully avoided, however, is the one that might arise between parents.

There are two places where financial combat can get particularly ugly, with long-term lingering aftereffects. Both have to do with a spouse. The first occurs when parents are separated or divorced. There are already going to be bad feelings related to who pays for what. Mom and Dad can easily let this scuffle spill over into the realm of child-rearing, and how they are going to manage college expenses. If you can't work this out together amicably, you'll end up getting attorneys involved, or your son or daughter may have to try to finance school on his or her own. You don't want that. Be civil. Figure out a payment system that is fair to everyone. Avoid being vindictive. There is enough bad blood already.

Even married couples engage in funding fights regarding college costs. Nearly all couples have a tendency to fight over money. The lenient one can't understand why the other is not picking up more of the tab. The other fights off feeling like a money grubber and gets defensive. The stage is then set for some real knockdown drag-outs.

Instead, sit down and have a heart-to-heart talk with your spouse or partner. Your kid is either out of the house or soon will be, while your significant other probably will be around for a much longer period of time. College comes and goes. It won't be long until you and your mate are holding hands, smiling warmly at the graduation ceremony. So keep the peace until then.

Remember, when your child graduates, both parents will probably want to attend graduation, whether they are together or separated in some way. Both will want to feel as if they contributed to the child's success. Share the burden so you can share the joy later. College is no time to force your kid into some kind of mediator role, or to have him or her caught in between parents. In other words, *survival* is the key word once again. When it comes to dollars and all the emotions they generate, it's the best you can do.

11

Parents Day and Other Ordeals

One bright, clear, beautiful autumn day during your son or daughter's freshman year, an uncalled-for intrusion invades. Instead of mowing the lawn, raking a few leaves, watching a favorite football team on television, canning food from the garden, or any other of a variety of calming, pleasant weekend experiences, you will be required to attend Parents Day at your kid's college. What a gyp. In all the universe, only those who endlessly seek punch and cookies are going to get excited about this little collegiate hurdle.

The purposes of Parents Day are pretty obvious. The school wants Mom and Dad to feel a part of the university experience in some way. They want kids to feel natural and comfortable with having their folks around. In fact, Parents Day is supposed to be a heartwarming occasion during which the whole family bonds with each other and with the institution, making it an ideal time to get everyone thinking about giving back, through donations to the college, now and in future years. Table 11.1 summarizes the essential elements of one of these events.

Consider Parents Day from the perspectives of those involved—parents, students, and faculty. What quickly emerges is a portrait of uneasiness, painted in the colors of politeness and civility. Not exactly what the counseling staff had in mind.

TABLE 11.1
A Typical Parents Day Program

9:00 A.M.–10:00 A.M.	Coffee, punch, cookies while you stand around and make mindless conversation with faculty and students
10:00 A.M.–11:00 A.M.	"Rousing" speeches by administrators (yeah, right)
11:00 A.M.–12:00 noon	Campus tour led by your kid or some talented student tour guide
12:00 noon–1:00 P.M.	Lunch in the cafeteria (except for those smart enough to leave campus in pursuit of actual food)
1:00 P.M.–1:30 P.M.	Pep rally (only frustrated former cheerleaders enjoy this session)
1:30 P.M.–4:30 P.M.	Football game, watching your kid's inept team lose 42–6
approximately 3:00 P.M.	Half-time, during which parents are introduced *en masse* and get to stand up
4:30 P.M.	Walk back to the car, cough up a few bucks, and say goodbye. (Your child is, by now, short of funds, especially if he or she bought your lunch.)
5:00 P.M.	Parents drive home in exhausted silence or mumbling to themselves. Students head to Happy Hour, relieved.

The Parents. Two categories of parents are present. One group went to college and the other did not. Those who sent to college have the most common reaction: boredom. They've seen dorm rooms before. They remember what a cafeteria looks like. Looking back at classrooms elicits a mixture of anger (about a professor who jerked someone around back in college), relief (that they don't have to go there anymore), and regret (about that wonderful man or woman whom they never summoned the courage to ask out on a date). As far as seeing a classroom and relating that to what their youngster is currently experiencing, well, it probably doesn't happen.

Perhaps the most interesting aspect of this day for parents who were former students is the trip to the dorm room or Greek house, where they will discover that a full-fledged renovation process has taken place. The new decor reflects what kids believe their parents think a college student's room should look like. Most experienced parents know, however, that just a few hours before they arrived on campus, the room contained:

- empties
- posters peeling off the wall
- butt-filled ashtrays
- quizzes with grades of F on them
- love letters
- trash
- CDs lying everywhere
- unmade beds, maybe even without sheets
- a carelessly displayed contraceptive device

This technique, hiding the goods—called "impression mangement" in later life—is the beginning of training for putting on airs. For now, it's just good common sense. If your child doesn't bother to make this effort, you have another issue to consider: his or her casual disregard for your feelings. In either case, those who have attended college aren't usually so ancient that the institution seems foreign. Rather, it's merely inconvenient to have to be there.

The second type of parent didn't go to college. This group subdivides once more into parents who are thrilled the child is in school, making the attempt to go higher and farther in life and those who think college is mostly a waste and that professors are nothing more than "educated idiots."

Those who are thrilled will "ooh and aah" more than the norm. They actually want to meet the faculty and administrators and see the whole campus. Visiting the dorm room or Greek house brings tears to their eyes as they ponder their "baby" grown up and moving on to new heights. This kind of parent embarrasses the child no end.

Not looking naive is a big deal to an eighteen-year-old. A gawking dad is the epitome of dorkness. A smothering mom is an excruciating pain. Underneath this exterior of embarrassment, however, rests the heart and soul of a youngster who is probably more thrilled, and more proud, than you can imagine. They just can't show it.

The other type of parent, who thinks professors are educated idiots, arrives on campus with a major chip on his or her (usually his) shoulder. This parent often is a self-made success who thinks the only education that actually counts occurs on the job. He sees no need for his kid to take general education classes like art or drama. He figures these classes are useless, and no one is going to convince him otherwise. The child, in his or her Psychology 101 class, will learn about Sigmund Freud, who suggested that *projection* is a typical way for adults to deal with anxiety. The youngster will probably realize that the argumentative parent accusing every faculty member of being haughty is actually the most haughty person in the room.

The hostility exhibited by a parent who did not go to college is understandable. College life is quite foreign to someone who has never experienced a campus. The university atmosphere may also seem threatening. Without admitting it, the parent is aware that the professors, whom they call idiots, have knowledge, information, technology, and techniques beyond the comprehension of the average person. And who wants to feel average (or less)?

Unfortunately, the new freshman is often the one who has to bear the brunt of parental attacks on the institution. He or she is not able, and probably not willing, to offer a strong defense of the college. Significant others (the spouse of the critical parent, siblings of the freshman) should try to be certain the student does not suffer as a result of this form of parental ill will.

For all types of parents, there is one common experience: Everyone is going to be struggling for things to talk about. The student seeks topics that might at least mildly entertain the parents, while the parents try their best to look interested. Uncomfortable silences punctuate the day for the bulk of new college parents and their sheepish college newcomers. There are, of course, some college parents who truly enjoy returning to campus and seeing their kids.

These Ozzie and Harriet types are the ones who keep college administrators believing Parents Day is a good idea, as they watch Mom and Dad embracing and happily chatting with Junior or Missy. In other words, these annoying people mess it up for everyone else!

The Students.   College freshmen, if they are at all normal, have probably been through a gauntlet of changes which redefined their relations with you over the past decade. Early on, parents were just the greatest people in the world. This Mom-and-Dad-as-hero-and-heroine stage ended in the early teenage years, when being seen with parents suddenly became a dreaded experience—but the kid still needed rides to and from all their activities. Thus began the Mom-and-Dad-as-embarrassing-chauffeurs stage. Later teenage years brought strife, conflict, insubordination, and the Mom-and-Dad-as-tyrants-and-meddlers stage.

Now, time and distance has allowed everyone's heart to grow a little fonder. Parents Day may very well mark the first parent/offspring contact in quite a while. The college student, naturally, doesn't know exactly how to act. Your kid probably figures he should display a certain amount of deference; after all, these people (you) are paying some (or all) of the bill. Still, he is feeling more grown up, having fended for himself in many ways. The net result is a situation in which the parent-child relationship is being redefined one more time. You can help this process along. You can praise your kid's independence, take interest in his activities, and generally see to it that your interaction takes on a more mature form. This, you can hope, will be the beginning of the Mom-and-Dad-as-supportive-college-parents stage. Table 11.2 lists the kinds of things supportive moms and dads don't say on Parents Day.

Remember that changes in the parent-child relationship mean periods of readjustment for you as well. Face it: You liked being the hero, but knew it had to end. You smirked when they acted like they'd die if seen in your presence. You battled tenaciously during the insurgency period. Now, it's time to move on. Conjure up images of interacting with other young adults whom you did not raise during the past eighteen years. For the most part it is possible to converse comfortably with people who are about that age. Now try to do the same with your own child on Parents Day. Use the occasion to help

---

TABLE 11.2
What Not to Say on Parents Day

"Are you eating your vegetables?"

"I hope you're trying to meet a *nice* girl."

"Have you been taking your vitamins? You look tired."

"You need a haircut."

"I brought your pajamas. You forgot them when you moved."

"Stand up straight. You don't want your teachers seeing you slouch."

"Just because your friends go to the bar doesn't mean you have to."

"You're losing weight. Look, Henry, he's losing weight."

"You're gaining weight. Look at your daughter, Henry. Doesn't she look heavier?"

"So, have you wasted all your money yet?"

"Put on some clothes. You're half naked."

"Are you getting enough rest? You have bags under your eyes."

---

strengthen your relationship with your own budding young adult. Sure, it's a long shot, but so what? You're there. Make the best of the situation.

The Faculty. It's tough enough for parents to give up a Saturday morning. Consider the poor faculty members. What did they do to deserve this? They have the same lawns to mow, leaves to rake, football games to watch, gardens to tend, and so forth, but some compelling force (personal or otherwise) causes them to take the time to make the trip down to the campus. Many know they're supposed to be there, so they stand around awkwardly and try making small talk at the greeting session. These conversations become especially stilted when the teacher remembers that the student is earning a D, and is uncertain as to whether or not the parents know—or when the professor doesn't recognize the student at all, because he hasn't been to class!

A few professors truly enjoy the opportunity to interact with parents. They heartily hail the surprised mom and dad and throw them for a loop by recalling seemingly minor details about their particular youngster. Such warmhearted members of the faculty are rumored to come from other planets. Normal people aren't that nice.

The sad truth is, many parents find that the early morning mixer with the faculty is in fact the best part of the day. Once the administration rolls in, people start checking their shoes, because it quickly begins to feel like they've wandered into something pretty deep, dark, and sticky.

A few important matters can be discussed with professors who show up on this day. Ask them about your child's class attendance and attentiveness, and pose a few other mild-mannered questions along those lines. Be sure to inquire when your kid is off getting you a coffee refill. If a professor seems particularly enamored of your youngster, find out if he or she believes your young collegian could major in the professor's specialty. Think both in terms of aptitude and attitude. At the same time, don't ask about:

- grades (they aren't carrying their gradebooks)
- who your child is dating
- politics
- the football team (many professors couldn't care less)

Parents should remember that these faculty members are the ones who chose to attend. Showing courtesy and appreciation is a good idea, and it is possible to have some fairly intriguing dialogues in these circumstances. In some cases, alumni moms and dads get to reconnect with favorite old profs. There are worse fates.

Sibling Days

Some schools host another day of family bonding called Sibling Day, during which younger brothers and sisters visit as guests of the school and of the elder sibling. These events are transparent attempts to begin the recruiting process relatively early in the sibling's life.

You, as a parent, might wish to view Sibling Day as "Golden

Opportunity Day." The possibilities are exhilarating. You may have the house *all to yourselves,* as many times Sibling Day involves an overnighter! The college-student son or daughter gets to play campus big shot, thereby boosting a flagging ego and having a chance to bond with brother or sister. Besides, your children need some time to discuss their parents' increasingly abnormal behaviors by themselves. You'll be accused of going through "mental pause," among other maladies. Detailed descriptions of your cluelessness must occur. Quality bonding between members of this generation helps ensure family continuity for years to come. All this comes courtesy of some college recruiter, who simply needs warm bodies to fill classrooms in the future.

Most important, these days put college in the minds of younger brothers and sisters. Possibly they will begin to think about *which* college to attend, rather than *if* they will go at all. It's never too soon to encourage that mindset.

When you stop and think about it, Parents Days, Sibling Days, and all the other kinds of days colleges hold are rather flattering. After all, not everyone gets a day just for them. The comedian Red Buttons used to talk about all the people who "never got a dinner." Same idea. *Some people never get a day.* The secret is to be prepared, go with the flow, enjoy the situation, get what you can out of the presentations and tours, and embrace the chance to see your child. College goes by quickly, and this is one time to take a few pictures, see a few sights, and watch with wonder as this rambunctious and annoying teenager transforms into a pretty neat adult. Not bad for one day.

12

Surviving General Education
and Choosing a Major

Most college programs have one frustrating process in common. School officials take kids who are all pumped up about studying a particular subject and then make them wait for nearly two years of school before allowing them to pursue it. It isn't clear whether this approach is meant to teach students to deal with frustration, delay gratification, put up with b.s., or simply to provide a more well-rounded education. For whatever reason, that's the way it works.

Ordinarily, during the first two years of college, the bulk of the classes are labeled *general education,* liberal arts, foundation courses, or something similar. To the casual observer, these sessions may look like a kind of academic holding pattern. Or, they may appear to be sifting and sorting devices designed to eliminate students from the university, so that individual majors don't get clogged up with too many pupils. In point of fact, there is a small amount of truth to each of these characterizations.

The general education portion of a degree program is oriented toward several objectives. These include:

Exposure to a wide variety of academic disciplines.   Most young people have not chosen a major by the time they arrive on campus. Even some of those who think they know what their major will be may discover a far more interesting field of study while taking general education classes. General ed programs present a series of alternatives, so new students can make more reasoned choices.

Educating the whole person. Although this may seem like a high-falutin' academic bromide, a general education program has an important function. A well-rounded student is knowledgeable about more than the technical aspects of a particular major. Being a college-educated person is supposed to mean that one's general level of knowledge is expanded. If the college truly does the job right, its graduates understand not only specific bodies of knowledge, but also possess the ability to think critically and apply reasoning processes to various problems and circumstances. General ed programs should provide the major groundwork for these skills.

Establishment of an academic track record. The GPA (grade point average) can be used to steer unqualified students out of the school, or to keep them out of majors in colleges where they must apply for admission to a degree program. As has always been the case, one objective of grades is to generate a ranking of students. In spite of the pervasive problem of inflated grades, educators, employers, and even parents still want to know who's doing better (or worse) than whom in the classroom.

The standard general education program consists of four to six key areas. Within these areas, students may choose specific classes to take. An average liberal arts or general ed program requires courses in the following areas:

Basic Skills courses include Math, English, and Communications. Typical classes in Math include Algebra, College Math, Trigonometry, Calculus, Math for the Numbers-Impaired, and Math for the Ridiculously Smart.

English begins with standard introductory classes, including Composition and Writing, Literature, and Research Writing. (An introduction to pompousness by faculty also normally occurs in these courses.) Conventional communications courses include Speech (that is, talking in front of a crowd) and Business Communications (talking to business people).

Humanities incorporates Art, Music, Theater, Foreign Languages, History, and Philosophy together. Art courses consist of Drawing, Painting, Sculpture, Crafts, and Art Appreciation (appreciating others who draw, paint, sculpt, or craft). Music courses are Chorus, Band, Music Literature (music theory and criticism), Music History, and Music Appreciation (appreciating others who play or sing). Theater courses include Acting, Stage Design, Technical Theater, and, of course, the inevitable Theater Appreciation.

Foreign Language programs vary depending on the school. The most common language courses offered are French, Spanish, Latin (for preseminary programs) and German. Some schools offer courses in Japanese, Chinese, Russian, and other languages. If your child is interested in enhancing employment opportunities after graduation, encourage him or her to learn a foreign language.

History classes can be about the United States, Europe, Africa, Asia, Latin America, World Civilization, or The History of Everything Else. Philosophy courses usually focus on ethics and logic, and are where, as Bill Cosby pointed out years ago, students can ask questions like "Why Is There Air?"

Social and Behavioral Sciences include Psychology, Sociology, Political Science, Anthropology, Geography/Demography, and interdisciplinary courses such as Women's Studies or Chicano studies. Psychology courses are either introductory courses or about Abnormal Psychology. Most kids should take Abnormal, to learn more about themselves.

Sociology classes include Introduction to Sociology and Advanced Sociology, but no one really knows how to tell when you've become advanced. Political Science professors examine politics and government at the state, local, or national level. Bomb-making and dirty tricks are for juniors and seniors. Geography is the study of turf. Demography is analysis of the people who occupy a certain section of turf.

Anthropology is the investigation of human cultures and traits. Most colleges don't offer this as a major, but rather just as a support for other programs, which aggravates anthropology profs to no end. (Being annoyed is part of the culture of college teaching, after all.) Women's Studies means studying women in society and in various cultures.

Physical and Life Sciences are exactly what their names imply. Chemistry and Physics are physical sciences. In many schools you can get through this requirement by taking a course in Geology, the study of rocks. Life Sciences consist of Biology, Ecology, Zoology, Botany, and Physiology.

Physical Fitness consists of both Physical Education and Health classes. It's true: you still can't get out of most colleges without a class in P. E.

There may be other basic subject areas required by some institutions, but those included in the five groups above are still the most common ones offered in most general ed programs. As a parent, you should realize that most freshmen and sophomores won't show strong interest in these classes, even though they may be among the more engaging subjects a person can study. This is not to say that the kids won't learn anything. Besides a modicum of new knowledge, they will most likely acquire the skills listed in Table 12.1

TABLE 12.1
Skills Students Develop in General Education Classes

- dozing without snoring
- looking interested while daydreaming
- skipping class without getting caught—or without grades being affected
- scoping out body parts without being obvious
- flirting while taking notes
- checking the clock every thirty seconds, while hiding the frustration that time is not passing faster
- enjoying the autumn or spring weather vicariously by looking out the window
- unobtrusively scratching graffiti into a desktop
- knowledge about how to appreciate stuff

So, without fanfare, the masses meander through general education courses. With luck, somewhere along the way your youngster will acquire a new interest in a subject he or she knew little or nothing about before college. In addition, you have to hope for at least decent grades. When general education succeeds, students evolve into better citizens, become aware of a wider world, think about things more analytically and carefully, and are at an advantage at dinner or cocktail parties because they don't talk the usual drivel. In spite of these benefits, most kids take the low road and get by with as little effort as possible. As a result, the items in Table 12.2 soon apply.

TABLE 12.2
General Ed Memories

What They Won't Remember in Two Years

- the professor's name
- the title of the course
- any subject matter of note

What They Will Remember

- the person they sat beside but never summoned the courage to ask out (which they will regret again at a future Parents Day, when they revisit the campus to see a daughter or son)
- any D or F grade
- getting caught daydreaming, resulting in a snide comment by the professor

---

One of the newer trends in education is to try to cultivate an interest in what is called "lifelong learning" through general education classes. Unfortunately, Table 12.2 more closely approaches reality.

Choosing a Major

It's easy to tell when general education courses begin to wind down. What will be left are the classes students truly dread. Think about how your kids ate dinner. They always saved the spinach, lima beans, and all of those other nasty things for last. It works the same way in school. In any case, when these onerous general ed classes are nearly completed, during the second semester of the sophomore year a student must actually commit to a more specific course of study: the college major.

For the most part, a major consists of thirty to sixty hours of coursework (12–20 classes), with increasing levels of specialization as the prefix number assigned to the course rises. A typical course numbering system is as follows:

100 level	mostly general education courses for freshmen; those barely breathing ordinarily pass
200 level	general ed classes for sophomores; designed to eliminate students who are truly unready or unable to perform
300 level	normally the first tier of courses offered for juniors in a major
400–600 level	advanced classes for seniors. (in schools that offer master's programs, 500 and 600 numbers are for both seniors and introductory master's students)

Hopefully, undeclared students—those with no already developed idea about which major to choose—will have settled on a preference usually by the end of the second year. Those who chose a major long ago have been chewing at the bit to get started. Choosing a major boils down to the one question that few young adults feel ready to answer: *What do you want to do with the rest of your life?*

No pressure there. Parents typically pound their kids with this query for years before college. Who really knows? Take comfort in what many university recruiters tell incoming freshmen: Most people who are now eighteen will change *careers* three times during their adult lives. In many cases, the job they will eventually end up with may not even *exist* right now. Consequently, selecting almost any major probably makes sense, in one way or another. Retraining and retooling will be a natural part of the workaday world in the coming years and for the next generation. So, tell your kid to relax and make the most of whatever course of study he or she chooses while in school.

When it comes to options, the possibilities seem endless. Table 12.3 is a brief review of some of the most popular majors. Each is accompanied by examples of one or more jobs the major might lead to.

TABLE 12.3
Majors and Employment

Major	Career	Worst Case
Accounting	company accountant auditor	IRS agent
Art	graphic designer artist	starving artist
Biology	physician biologist	germ-warfare technician
Chemistry	lab chemist research chemist	mad scientist
Communications	producer publicist editor	spokesman for used- car dealership
Computer Science	data analyst programmer	hacker video-game addict
Drama	actor theater technician director	stage mom
Economics	government economist economics professor	U.S. budget director
Elementary Education	grade-school teacher	substitute teacher
Engineering	engineer	engineer on Disney train ride
English	writer literary critic professor of English	comic-book critic
Fashion Merchandising	buyer designer	thrift-shop fashion coordinator

Finance	banker chief financial officer	savings and loan officer
French	interpreter translator teacher	rude maître d'
General Studies	jack-of-all-trades	jack-of-all-trades
German	interpreter translator teacher	cook
Health	fitness or health instructor	"before" model for exercise equipment
History	historian	futurist
Home Economics	consumer advocate dietician	fry cook at a fast-food place
Insurance	insurance adjuster actuary	insurance sales rep
Journalism	news reporter editor	correspondent for *Entertainment Tonight*
Kinesiology	sports trainer physical therapist	massage-parlor owner
Library Science	librarian information broker archivist	file clerk
Management	manager	non-manager
Marketing	sales manager market researcher	phone answerer on QVC channel
Mathematics	mathematician	numbers runner
Military Science	military officer state trooper	unarmed security guard
Music	musician music teacher	composer of rap-music commercials
Nursing	registered nurse head nurse	bedpan coordinator

Ophthalmology	Ophthalmologist	professional focus group member
Paralegal Studies	paralegal legal assistant	bail bond clerk
Physics	physicist physics technician	toy designer for fast food kid meals
Political Science	attorney elected official	Rush Limbaugh's agent
Psychology	clinical psychologist researcher psychologist	normal, average guy
Recreation	recreation director fitness instructor	sign-in clerk at the Y
Secondary Education	high school teacher high school principal	high school janitor
Social Work	personal counselor caseworker	bartender receptionist
Spanish	interpreter translator teacher	bullfighter
Technology: Automobile Plastics Construction	auto technician plastics technician contractor	gas station attendant landfill custodian wrecker
Theology	clergyperson theologian	cult leader

Parents find that the inclination to intervene in the selection of a major is overwhelming. It's only natural to want your youngster to major in whatever was your major, way back when, or to believe that you know best what he or she should choose for a major. Resist the urge to impose. Answer inquiries if asked directly, patiently and subtly steer, but don't press!

A significant part of the process of growing up is learning how to make decisions on your own. Sometimes this means goofing up, badly. It takes strength to watch your kids make what you believe to be foolish judgments without becoming bossy and overdirective. Be strong. Let them spread their wings.

As a parent, your role is to give advice regarding the selection of a major, minor, or double major, without being too pushy. Subtle messages are best. For instance, you can introduce your child to people you know who have succeeded in the same major you want to suggest as an option. It's also fair to point out the difficulties associated with certain majors, so long as you also refer to their potential benefits.

Double Majors: The Overachiever's Option

About one out of every twenty students in college decides that one major is not enough. The end result is the classic double major. This option should be reserved for only the most serious, hard-charging, capable collegians. There are some benefits to having a double major. They include:

- in-depth knowledge of more than one subject
- more job prospects
- a better chance of entering a quality graduate program
- new insights into a given profession
- bragging rights for parents

In exchange, students and their parents will have to pay extra for these advantages. Although they only need one set of general ed classes, students with double majors must take prerequisite courses for both majors. Ordinarily this adds at least one semester of study. In addition, students with double majors tend to take *overloads,* or more than the allowable number of classes for regular students. College administrators, money hounds that they are, charge extra tuition for overloads. Either the parent or the student will have to pick up the tab. Also, administrators normally insist that students with overloads must maintain higher GPAs than their peers. Thus, only highly motivated students should even consider taking a double major.

As parents, one of your concerns should be in the area of R & R if your child decides to attempt a double major. Your youngster's college career should include having some fun, playing, and enjoying campus life. Students with a double majors may end up substituting long hours in labs, libraries, and study halls for the more enjoyable elements of college. Poor time managers especially are prone to not seeing the light of day. If you think your daughter or son would be swamped by having a double major, make sure he or she gives it careful consideration before making such a move. Explain that you do indeed want him or her to have some fun while in school.

Also, check to make certain all the effort is going to pay off. Be aware that many students with double majors end up spending an extra semester or year in school, or take numerous summer courses to finish both programs. Is the wait worth it? Only you and he or she can decide that for sure. Double-majoring is no big deal to a select few students. Others find that it makes their life miserable than the benefits received. Not only that, but there is another option.

The College Minor

Minors are like vice presidents. For the most part, they seem inconsequential. They work behind the scenes, never grabbing the glory that the president (the college major) gets. Still, they can be very useful.

A college minor normally consists of approximately six to eight classes (18 to 24 college hours) designed to provide strong exposure to a subject without making it the major course of study. Minors are great support mechanisms. Wonderful combinations can be created, matching a student's interests or talents with his or her major field of study. For example, art can be linked to business, sports to communication, English to history, and psychology to chemistry. There are literally dozens of other possibilities that connect a student's unique talents to a major course of study.

In contrast to double majors, minors are more easily assimilated into a traditional college program. The student may end up in a few summer courses (see chapter 13) or have larger class loads in the final two years of school, but most find a minor to be fairly easily managed.

Parents normally can respond with enthusiasm to the selection of a minor. Only when the minor seems likely to take away time or energy from the major should parents discourage their youngsters from taking one. College can and should be a great time to develop new or long-standing interests, and to engage in activities that inspire academic passions. Minors provide excellent outlets for these energies.

In most universities and colleges, neither minors nor second majors are required of any student. Both of these options are available to students with special interests and those who wish to enhance their career prospects.

Changing Majors: What to Expect

Your kid's choice of a major would be a much more dramatic event, were it not for the fact that so many college students change their minds! Once, twice, even three times in a four-year period, they may rethink the direction they have taken. As a parent, you can think of these moments as one more chance to let them guide their own lives, with you as supporter rather than pilot.

It may not be a constitutional right, but Americans believe they have the inalienable prerogative to change their minds. Wasn't it Emerson who wrote, "A foolish consistency is the hobgoblin of little minds?" (Yes, it was.)

First, there are small changes. These are manifested in the adding and dropping of classes. Students add classes when something suddenly looks interesting or necessary, at the last minute, after the semester has already started. Normally there is some paperwork and a small fee to pay for changing a schedule. It's not a big deal at all, and parents should treat it that way.

Dropping classes, on the other hand, results from numerous dilemmas and decisions, some of which may indeed require your attention. The most ominous is a drop resulting from bad grades. One of the major contributors to grade inflation is a school policy that allows for an eleventh-hour drop of a class, even when the student is about to receive a failing grade. In place of the F the student was headed toward, an innocuous WP (withdrew—passed),

WF (withdrew—failed), or a simple Withdrew appears on the grade card or transcript. Since the zero point value associated with an F does not enter into the calculation, the overall GPA remains at a higher level.

Parents should be most concerned with the why's and how's of a bad-grade-related drop. Was it lack of interest or lack of effort? Was it lack of preparation? When you find out about a last-minute class drop, you may want to have a heart-to-heart talk with your youngster. It's your job to encourage the academically overwhelmed or just plain lackadaisical student into making a better effort. If the main problem seems to be laziness or a preoccupation with social life, you should feel free to use tactics—including financial incentives and threats—that are certain to get your son or daughter's attention.

If a lack of background, inability, or a simple mismatch with a given professor in a specific course results in dropping a course, you may be able to help solve the problem. It may be just a matter of getting your daughter to climb back on the horse that threw her off. You may need to reassure your son that taking background or remedial courses is not something to be ashamed of, but rather is a sign of maturity and of the will to succeed, regardless of the obstacles.

There are other reasons why students drop courses, ranging from things as mundane as, not liking the class to feeling swamped and needing to reduce one's load. As far as you're concerned, these situations are best handled on a drop-by-drop basis. If you start to see a pattern developing, however, in which courses are dropped every semester, it may be a symptom of a more serious problem. Your child may be:

- taking on too much, and needing to fall back as a result
- too picky
- starting strong, but unwilling to finish a semester's work
- having roommate problems
- experiencing romantic problems
- encountering something quite serious, such as alcohol or drug abuse problems

Be watchful. A certain amount of adding and dropping classes is normal. Only excesses should be investigated.

In the end, choosing a college major is like visiting a hairdresser. Sometimes the hairstyle is great, but it just doesn't fit your particular head. Sometimes the stylist does sloppy work and shouldn't have been chosen in the first place. Every once in a while, there is a great match of style and substance, or coiffeur and coiffée. The great thing about haircuts and majors is that they don't last forever, and you can always change them.

Switching majors, however, does tend to extend a person's stay in school. The prerequisite classes that support one major may not apply to another. Therefore, a person who has changed majors more than once normally ends up taking extra courses and credit hours. Sometimes the additional load results in the student being forced to stay in school an extra semester or year in order to graduate. In other instances it's possible to catch up by attending summer classes or interim (between fall and spring semester) courses.

There is one other case to examine when it comes to a college career—that of the individual who has so totally failed in a particular major that he or she has gone beyond academic probation, to suspension. Yes, it's true; a college can still, in some instances, flunk kids out of school for poor academic performance.

Even then there is an option. Many universities allow for what is known as *academic bankruptcy*. This means that the student is permitted to start over, with a clean slate. Administrators and faculty recognize that sometimes a person may be immature, unprepared, or overwhelmed by personal circumstances, and flunk out of college as a result. Academic bankruptcy is a tough road, but if the student is determined, it is a pathway out of some pretty dire scholarly circumstances.

Parents are an intrusive group. They think they know what is best, and many times they do. At the same time, parents should remember their own histories, and how leaving the nest was part being pushed out and part struggling to be free. So it must be with all of these tough college and career choices. If you want your kids to soar with the eagles, they sometimes first have to plummet like a rock. If they take off in immediate flight and rise to heights higher than you ever imagined, document it. You want all the evidence you can get when you brag to your friends!

13

Holidays and Vacations

The human mind is a wonderful thing. Among two of its greatest virtues are the abilities to forget and to forgive. Once your young collegian matriculates and actually stays in school for a time, you start to forget. You forget loud music and constant refrains of "Close the door," "Clean up that mess," "Turn it down," along with the always inspiring, "This is our house, and while you live here you'll follow our rules!"

You forget the arguments and the anger. You forget all your teenager's annoying little habits, like leaving wet towels on your brand-new carpet and never taking dishes to the sink after dinner (much less helping to wash them). You forget the mysterious language that you tried to translate to make sure your child wasn't using code words to conduct drug deals or to call you something outrageous or obscene. Soon enough, you may find yourself actually missing your kid. You may even catch yourself saying, "It wasn't really *so* bad having him home"—unless, of course, there are others in your brood still at home serving as continual reality checks.

As the memories of high school traumas fade, it also becomes much easier to forgive, to let go of the anger and mellow into a contented state of being. Then comes the fateful moment. You begin to actually *look forward* to their visit. Big mistake. Holidays and summer vacations are, in many ways, invasions. Your sense of tranquillity, your new routines, and, in general, your way of life will be disrupted when Joe College or Susie Sorority returns home. It's best to be prepared, so here are some things to think about.

Thanksgiving Day

The first sign of things to come takes place in November. Most kids have been gone for three months or so, and now they are coming home. Actually, Thanksgiving is not as bad as other visits will be, as most parents are still in that calm, forgiving, and forgetful mode, and the student's stay is short.

The typical Thanksgiving visit starts with students cutting classes early in the week to get an extra day or two of break. Thus, if the college releases students just for Thursday and Friday, most kids leave campus on Wednesday morning. If the university gives them Wednesday free, they leave on Tuesday morning. If the school eliminates Tuesday classes, they might as well write off the whole week.

In addition, professors with any savvy know that Thanksgiving week is a bad time to schedule quizzes, tests, or due dates for term papers. These wise individuals are aware that insisting on preholiday deadlines makes students mad. Resentful students, who have memories like elephants, are going to be uncharacteristically eloquent in their course evaluations, making the professor look like a bad teacher. Who needs that? So, most faculty members give kids a breather; this, in turn, makes it an easy week for the faculty member. The people who bear the brunt of this system are the parents.

Eventually the moment of arrival is upon you. Your child will stand at the door, wondering if it's now appropriate to knock before entering or simply to walk in. Most choose the casual approach and open the door without signaling first. Startled, you jump about ten feet in the air, quickly trying to recover your dignity on the way down. Mom tends to reach the child first and, being Mom, drops her guard and hugs him or her excitedly. Sons ponder the *hugging versus handshake* dilemma when Dad appears on the scene. Work out the greeting process on your own. Some families hug, some shake hands, others put their hands in their pockets and either say "hello," "hi," or "howdy," depending on geographic region. None of these greetings is bad or good. Each is related to the customs and confort zone of the household in question.

Soon the standard small talk begins. "How was your trip?" is always a good starter, along with "How are your classes going?" Expect awkward silences. They don't know exactly how to talk to you, and vice versa. It will take some time to get more free-flowing conversation going. Later in the visit, these quiet first few hours may seem like a blessing.

As you greet your child, be aware that both you and he or she probably are experiencing a surge of conflicting emotions. The youngster may feel out-of-place, nostalgic, happy, strange, sad, enthusiastic, and bewildered, all at once. You will probably feel old. After all, a physical reminder of the passing years now stands or sits before you.

At first, conversation tends to center on grades and classes, friends and family. It should be relatively easy to stay away from touchy subjects, like politics and money.

It won't be long, however, until your returning and conquering collegian starts to get on your nerves. First he will dump about two month's worth of dirty clothes on the laundry room floor and expect Mom to take care of it! Then he'll slam down some dinner and take off to go be with his friends. This hurts a little, because parents see their low ranking on the priority pole demonstrated in clear terms. Making things worse in a hurry, the kid will stay out until some ridiculous hour. This not-so-gentle reminder of days gone by aggravates most moms and dads. It means most parents will have a restless night of sleep. (Only those who have learned to stop worrying about late nights will get a decent amount of rest.) This happens the day before the big Thanksgiving feast must be prepared!

Then, in order to drive the point home, a returning freshman will sleep until about, oh, *two in the afternoon*. She will wake up refreshed and perky just as you're starting to really get sleepy. Then she will bang around in the bathroom and generally annoy you.

This is standard college student operating procedure. Most

parents try hard to endure it peaceably. After all, it's Thanksgiving, and you want to enjoy your kid's company. You will try to ignore your initial level of disgust at his or her behavior and instead concentrate on football and food. After eating, everybody dozes. The family may be able to savor a little bit of time together.

Next comes the weekend. Late nights, phone calls, messes, and a general disdain for your parental authority return. Most parents are more than ready for Sunday to arrive, when the child goes back to campus. What remains after the Thanksgiving visit is a sense of impending gloom. If it was this testy over four or five days, what will Christmas break be like?

Fa, la, la, la, la...la, la, la, la

Today's young people don't remember Perry Como. They don't know the words to "I'll Be Home for Christmas." Nostalgia isn't a big deal. Consequently, a trip home for the holidays probably has a completely different meaning for kids than it has for parents.

Many psychologists have noted people's tendency to glamorize and idealize what they expect will happen over the Christmas holiday. Many folks expect family problems to disappear. They think everyone will simply mesh together in the soft glow of yuletide bliss. College parents are particularly susceptible to this error. Unfortunately, there are no picture-postcard holidays. Reality, in this case, is a little less warm and fuzzy than people think it will be. Table 13.1 is a quick summary of what you can expect from your returning college student during the Christmas holiday season. Sing it to the tune of "The Twelve Days of Christmas."

Christmastime is a tug-of-war between parent and student. The pulling and tugging expresses the continuing delineation of rights and privileges, responsibilities and duties, being negotiated between father and son, mother and daughter. In other words, they want to continue to trash the house, talk on the phone until all hours, come and go as they please, eat when they feel like it, sleep as late as they want, and in general treat you as if you are servants in their own personalized home motel—*and* they also want you to think of them and treat them as if they are adults!

TABLE 13.1
The Twelve Days of a College Parent's Christmas

12 late night outings

11 eves of dancing

10 drinking binges

 9 midnight phone calls

 8 claims of freedom

 7 angry outbursts

 6 temper tantrums

 5 …anguished wails

 4 "oops, I'm sorry"

 3 "please forgive me"

 2 cheapo presents

 1 "I love you, Mom and Dad" (only in senior year)

Meanwhile, they probably won't have given more than a vague thought to buying Christmas presents and will also be broke. Guess who gets hit up for a loan? Some collegians even express the opinion that parents *owe* them funds to purchase presents. Imagine that.

Expect to feel completely ambushed by this most recent development in their development. The most jarring impact occurs during Christmas of the freshman year, when—unless you are taking this book very, very seriously—you will not have prepared yourselves for this massive disruption to the tranquillity of your home. In the majority of households there will be at least one shouting match (if your family is the yelling-and-screaming type) or major disagreement (if your household uses the discussion-and-negotiation model) related to what you maintain are the rules versus what they think is fair.

A good method of dealing with this clash is to be prepared to point out the manner in which they are treating you. Tell them your feelings are hurt when they take you for granted. Assert that they are now—however beloved—only guests in your house. Remind them that being an adult consists not only of privileges, but also of demonstrating appropriate behaviors, one of which is being considerate of others, especially elders.

They're going to fire back with stuff about how you treat them like children, how you overanalyze, how you intrude too much into their personal lives, and so forth. Besides, this is their vacation, and they need to *relax*. Respond with the ever-popular, "This is our house, and while you're here you'll live by our rules." Then suggest that you're willing to change the rules, so long as they are willing to make even the semblance of effort to abide by them.

Beyond this major altercation over turf, you probably will try to enjoy their visit as much as you can. It is possible to catch up on what happened during the first semester of school, and to find out whether they feel comfortable with the college, their roommates, the town or city where the school is located, and other important matters. You want to find out if they're adjusting to campus life, and what their future plans might be. Some may even have a few ideas about a major (see chapter 12). In the saner moments of their stay, try to conduct these more important discussions.

There are other strategies to consider for dealing with the holidays as well. Here are a few ideas you may find helpful.

Leave. Most employers grant a day or two of leave around the holidays. If you can build up even a little bit of vacation time, you can normally string together New Year's Day with one or two other days, linked to a weekend. This means you can take off for a short trip to somewhere warm (or warmer) and get away from it all. You'll love it because the trip will break up the winter and let you unwind from the crush of the holiday season. Your college student will love it because he or she gets the house for a few days, alone. So what's a little property damage in exchange for some peace and quiet? Not only that, but ordinarily upon your return it will be only a matter of a few days until the new semester begins, and your son or daughter will be heading back to college.

The key to getting away is planning. Establish a Christmas Club or Holiday Club account, or simply save money. If you can set aside just $10 per week ($20 is better if you can afford it), you'll have more than $500 for a New Year's vacation, which, if nothing else, means you can book a couple of nights at a hotel or motel in a nearby city. Reserve early, since many other parents of college students may have the same idea. Parents of high school seniors must begin saving during the holiday season the year *before* their son or daughter starts college. The rest of you should have the system in place. The great advantage to this approach occurs during the time between Thanksgiving and Christmas. As you anticipate the impending reappearance of your college student, you can look at the brochures from your chosen resort to calm your nerves, and feel pleased that you've cut down on the strain of the upcoming season.

Get Them to Leave.   A second major approach to the Christmas dilemma is to encourage your youngster to have lots of overnighters with friends (they stay out until all hours anyway). Beyond that, you might even get them thinking about a midwinter road trip to somewhere nice but inexpensive. Cutting loose a few dollars to help with expenses is an investment in peace and quiet.

Still, you may be wary of any attempt they make to spend Christmas with a boyfriend or girlfriend. These arrangements are filled with landmines. They may decide to just live together from then on, elope, or do some other silly thing that will interfere with school.

Encourage them to work.   Some college students are able to find temporary jobs over the holidays. This approach yields two major benefits. First, they're not around as much, and second, they might build up a little spending money for second semester.

Schedule lots of events.   If neither you nor your collegian can leave, it's a good idea to plan as many social gatherings as you can. Besides a Christmas gala and a big New Year's Eve bash, you can plan bowling parties, card-playing soirees, football-watching binges, and as many activities as possible to get you, them, or everyone out of the house. Even movies can provide much-needed relief.

The secret to success for the mid-year break is *distractions,* both for you and for your college student. The more you can do to break the routine, keep yourself entertained, and dispel potential conflicts, the better off all of you will be.

For most parents, the two most challenging holidays are Thanksgiving and Christmas. There are however, other possible times of trouble lurking on the horizon.

Spring Break

Hormones are amazing things. They come and go, ebbing and flowing as the seasons pass and the person grows. Unfortunately, when those first few warm days of spring arrive and the sun hits the skin of college students, hormones become uncontrollable demons that take over their mental and physical being for weeks on end. In the midst of this hormone frenzy, they get a week off from college!

The question each mother and father must carefully consider is, "Do we want our child going through this troublesome time at home?" The answer is probably a resounding "Maybe, maybe not." If you live near a resort area and know they'll be at the beach or gone most of the time, then maybe. If you live in the frigid north, where no swimsuits come out until May or June, then maybe not. Many colleges offer formal or informal caravans during spring break that take college students to South Padre Island in Texas, Daytona Beach in Florida, Palm Springs in California, some other "snow bird" destination, or a ski resort. If you can afford it at all, and maybe even if you can't, send your son or daughter on one of these vacations.

Remember, sordid memories are part of college life. Young people that age need to debauch at least once during their school years. If you went to college, you probably remember more about a few key parties than you do about most of your classes. It's tough for Ma and Pa to let go. Parents tend to have "fun quotas" which they apply to their children. Even so, it doesn't hurt for a youngster to overdo for some brief time period. Just make sure they do their homework *before* they leave.

Spring breaks spent at home are boring and frustrating for most college students. They know their friends are out having a whole bunch of fun. Without falling into a keeping-up-with-the-Joneses syndrome, try to facilitate some frolic and merriment when spring break arrives. They'll be more grateful than you'll even imagine.

Thanksgiving, Christmas break, and spring vacations are challenging periods for parents and students. Successful management of these occasions will keep you from holding grudges the rest of the time while they're away. Always bear in mind that four years of college go by pretty quickly. If you can, stop and enjoy your brief time with them, and drink in their frustrations, victories, ambitions, and excitement as best you can. It won't be long until they'll be regular old boring adults, just like you. With luck, they'll soon be out of the house for good. Play your cards right and holidays can become the picture-postcard events you always thought they would be. If not, lay down the law, then duck!

Summertime...But the Livin' Ain't Easy

Hormonal surges don't go away when spring break ends. Many times, these lurid feelings only intensify with the onset of summer. All that skin begs to be looked at, kids have so much free time, and their minds are idle. Naturally their thoughts turn to things biological.

Consequently, parents of college kids must brace themselves for the impact of the summer season. Kids get used to a certain level of freedom during the school year. Parents, in turn, still probably believe there should be rules, restrictions, and all that other bogus stuff. When your college student returns home for the summer, conflicts are bound to emerge.

For Mom and Dad, the best course of action, as has been the case with other youthful intrusions, is to have a plan. You need to generate some appealing alternatives for your kid. Table 13.2 presents the activities of vacationing college students and what you will have to cope with all summer long.

TABLE 13.2
Favorite College Student Summer Activities

Tanning	Watching others tanning
Swimming	Watching others swimming
Sunbathing	Watching others sunbathing
Shopping for sunglasses (day)	Going to movies (night)
Fast-food junkets (day and night)	Hanging out (day and night)
Staying up all night	Sleeping all day

Notice what's missing from Table 13.2: Anything productive! It's your assignment to make sure your kid achieves a good balance between lying fallow, in order to be refreshed for the next school year, and not completely wasting three whole months. This is another tough job, but one parents cannot ignore.

Kids who go to college take one of two basic tacks when the regular school year ends. One group enrolls in summer classes. The other works. Each of these options has its pros and cons. You should try to have some input as to what option your kid chooses. Read on for some basic approaches and a few key tips.

Those Who Work

Working in the summer is an excellent option for many college students. There are some clear benefits, for them and for you. Working means they will:

- be out of the house for large blocks of time
- earn their own spending money
- keep busy, so they don't need as much spending money
- gain hands-on experience in a chosen major
- create an alternative outlet for flirting, so they aren't doing it on your telephone all day and night
- get tired (at least a little)
- generate a line for their résumés

By summertime, you will probably be broke from a year's worth of college expenses. So, you need help. If your youngster can at least be a break-even proposition over the summer (not save any money, but not cost any either), you can recoup and regroup for the next school year. It's even possible to devise some kind of contract with collegians, whereby they know in advance that they have to fund themselves through the hot summer months, in addition to saving some money for the start of the next school year. Also, your youngster will gain a greater sense of responsibility and possibly will feel that he or she is contributing, even if in a small way, to the family's financial well-being.

Helpful Hint No. 1. If your daughter or son works, make

absolutely certain the job has an early starting time, between 7:00 A.M. and 9:00 A.M. Why, you ask? Seasoned parents already know the answer to this one. It means the laborer will come home at night just a little bit earlier, at least part of the time. This bodes well for your ability to rest, and your sense of sanity. There's no avoiding the fact that they're going to have late-nighters throughout the summer, but if they have a regular day job there is at least a chance they'll get to bed early from time to time. The worst possible job is one that starts around noon and ends at 8:00 or 10:00 P.M. This allows your kid every opportunity to stay out until ridiculous hours all the time and then sleep in. You will constantly be awakened by their return in the middle of the night. Life is too short for that.

Kids who live and work at home during the summer are a major pain. First of all, they think that since they've been making their own rules all school-year long, and since they've got a few dollars in their pockets, they should have a big-time say in how things run in your house. This includes the hours they can come and go, mealtimes, and all other matters of turf and territory. During the summer, you will also quickly rediscover

- MTV and the Comedy Channel
- local rock stations
- constant phone calls
- channel surfing
- friends who just drop in
- squealing tires in the driveway
- interpersonal crises, especially those related to a current boy-friend or girlfriend, spinning a web of moodiness and despair

Another approach exists. It's possible to encourage your youngster to move in with a few friends. What you gain is some tranquillity throughout the summer months. What you lose is your kid's presence and most of the income they generate. In other words, breaking even is less likely. Instead, parents are hit up for all kinds of loans and freebies. Also, a trend is often established in which your child always seems to show up for a visit right around mealtime. Still, on balance, it may be best for your mental health to encourage your kid to live with college chums.

Summer jobs range from routine to complex. Believe it or not, many young people are better off taking what is essentially a mental vacation by doing something simple like waiting tables, shelving library books, or serving ice cream. The pressure and stress of college, which affects some students more than others, may best be relieved by some time when thinking isn't a major requirement. Besides, budding adults tend to appreciate money more when they feel that they've really earned it. Funds may be spent more carefully and are more likely to be saved. After the freshman and sophomore years, uncomplicated jobs such as those mentioned (lifeguarding or yard work) may be ideal.

As a college career progresses, opportunities to pursue a chosen vocation often appear. Internships, along with regular employment openings, may give your child a leg up on the competition in the job market, even before graduation. Having both the degree and some experience makes for a better application packet down the road.

A summer of work is good practice for later life, especially if the young workers get in the amount of play they need. Don't forget the incredible stamina twenty-year-olds possess. They can get by for quite a while with five hours of sleep per night. Therefore, don't worry too much about their exhaustion levels. Most college students really can take care of themselves by now.

Whether they stay at home or with friends in town, returning college freshmen, sophomores, and juniors who choose to work will change your lifestyle during the summer months. Not that it's all bad. Parents get to see how their kids have grown and matured over the previous year. Mom and Dad may be able to spend a little quality time with their youngsters.

Still, kids who come home to work during the summer have an awful lot of free time. They forget, unfortunately, that even though they have lots of idle hours, *you* still have to go to work. In other words, kids fail to remember to be quiet when they come staggering in at 3:00 A.M. After all, they've been staggering in all school year without bothering a soul. At the same time, they still manage to devote a considerable amount of the day to the pastimes listed in Table 13.2. Therefore:

Helpful Hint No. 2. Do all you can to keep them from over-tanning. Young people have a tendency to believe tans are sexy and otherwise harmless. Many bars and some social groups hold show-your-tan events and contests. This occurs despite the fact that dermatologists have documented, in more detail than ever, the extent to which suntanning permanently damages the skin. Young adults who tan and burn too much are taking an awful risk. This is one area in which you can do something tangible to help them in the long term. It may be necessary to do something really gross. For example, you could show them some skin cancer victims or simply the damage too much sun does over time by making skin appear leathery. Wrinkles and blotches don't look as sexy as the golden tan the kids are showing off now. It won't be pleasant to undertake this task, but it's worth it. Predictions are that skin cancer rates will skyrocket in the next decade. Do your part. Buy some sunscreen. Mom, nag. Dad, support Mom.

Those Who Go to Summer School

First, a quick reminder. Those who attend summer school *still come home,* at least for part of the time. The typical university calendar incorporates about two weeks off between graduation day and the start of the first summer session. This gives faculty members a needed break. Then there is normally an extended Fourth of July weekend and another two- to three-week period of free time following the close of summer school, before the first faculty meeting of the next college year. These breaks provide numerous opportunities for students to go home to freeload for a few days. This means you are not immune to the problems encountered during the hurricane season by parents of working college students.

Think first, therefore, about the good times—the days when kids are in class. There are several variations on summer school pro-grams. The more traditional ones offer two five-week sessions. The first summer session begins around June 1 and ends about July 8–10. The second session then starts immediately and ends around August 5. Classes presented in five-week sessions normally run about one hour each, five days per week, which means a typical student can take two courses per session. That's the equivalent of about one semester's worth of work (twelve credits, or four courses) during the summer. Some colleges shorten the two sessions to four-week offerings, which means classes run about one-and-a-half hours each, five days a week. Still, two courses per session totals four courses, if a student attends both sessions.

Many students and professors enjoy the opportunity to restrict their involvement in summer school to just one of the two sessions. This gives them about eight weeks off during prime vacation season! To parents, it means the kids will be gone for one month of summer, but home for the other two. Don't look a gift horse in the mouth. Take the one month and be happy. Besides, you can then insist that they work for the rest of the vacation season.

A third form of summer school is one eight-week session. Many colleges offer these courses on a four-day workweek basis. This gives faculty members eight three-day weekends in a row, which is good for professorial morale. Students enjoy the extra free day, which can be used for study or fun. Parents endure lots of visits from their kids, but at least have some respite Mondays through Thursdays. Eight-week sessions generally limit students to either two or three classes. The benefit is a leisurely pace and a relaxed learning atmosphere.

Several universities now schedule classes in *trimesters*, three 12-to-14-week sessions per year, rather than two semesters of 15 to 17 weeks each. Courses are offered on nearly a year-round basis. Even in these places, however, students are allowed time off.

Many schools also have added mini-course sessions. These intensive one- or two-week class periods (sometimes called *interim classes*) meet all day long. Interim or mini-courses are generally scheduled between the end of the spring semester and the start of summer school. A few colleges offer interim courses during the year-end winter break as well. Only students with a great deal of self-discipline and concentration should enroll in interim classes. These classes may be either prerequisite general ed courses or specialties within a major.

Students enroll in more traditional summer school courses for a variety of reasons. A few of the most common include:

- making up classes they dropped
- making up classes they flunked (to replace the grade)
- working ahead toward an earlier graduation date
- catching up, after falling behind, so they can graduate with their class
- taking special-interest courses they don't have time for during the regular school year
- enrolling in a particularly difficult class, so they can concentrate more on just the one subject
- reducing the number of hours needed during regular semesters
- making it possible to spend the summer on campus with a boyfriend or girlfriend
- becoming involved in special research projects

Helpful Hint No. 3.   As a parent, be sure your youngster is balancing his or her workload with fun, to avoid burnout. School is mentally draining for many students. If you sense she is starting to truly dread getting up and going to class, encourage her to take some time off to do something else. If you start to believe he will be more likely to drop out because he feels overwhelmed by school, tell him to consider working instead.

It has become more common for a college career to last for five and sometimes six years. Expect these delays. Know your youngster. If he or she is motivated and knows well in advance what major to choose, the four-year program with one summer on and a couple off will work just fine. Those who have false starts (changes in majors), double majors, or highly demanding majors may find that summer school can help them finish within four years.

Others may simply spend one more year on campus. Everyone knows that youth is wasted on the young, and that the young waste a lot of their youth. Extending college over an extra year may not be squandering time. In fact, it may be the best way for your child to finish school with higher grades and less stress. Talk to your new freshman or sophomore if you think a slower path to a degree will also be a better path. Help your child make the best choice for himself or herself, for now, all the while recognizing that things may change. Your goal is to help him or her obtain a degree, *not* to win some argument about time-management skills.

What About *Your* Life?

It's easy to forget that summer for a twenty-year-old takes place during *the same three months* as it does for you. Unless you already have abandoned all hope, you probably want to think about having some fun and relaxing a bit yourself. Extended weekends with visits to friends and relatives may be on your calendar. Longer trips to never-before-seen places or familiar fun spots may be on your agenda.

As a result, it's important for parents of college kids to make clearly reasoned decisions about how their own vacations proceed. For some, it may seem like a great idea to take your college student along for the ride. Many kids will truly appreciate being included and will be on their best behavior during the trip. Others are just petulant little troublemakers, and they should be left behind at all costs. Don't feel bad if that's the best resolution for your family.

Helpful Hint No. 4. Do a trial run. Take a three- or four-day trip to one of your child's favorite holiday places. If he or she reacts badly, you have your answer. Exclude him or her from all future vacations. On the other hand, if he or she adds to the merriment and enjoyment of the excursion, then you know he or she appreciates being included. Making plans early to take your college student along on your summer vacation gives everyone something to look forward to during the spring.

Always remember that you need to *have a life* while your son or daughter is in college. Whatever your summer routine used to be, keep it up. Some folks take long journeys to refresh themselves. Others prefer a series of shorter jaunts to revitalize their spirits. Don't let a youngster stop you from recharging your own batteries. It's your summer, too!

Handling Holiday and Summertime Confrontations

It's inevitable. They're going to make you mad. And, you're going to annoy them. So, what should be done? First and foremost, simply recognize that the potential for conflict exists. Both you and your child have become used to different patterns of living. It should come as no surprise that disagreements will arise—over money, use of your car, living arrangements, helping around the house, and how much authority you now hold.

Parents should realize that there is more than one way to skin a college cat. In the olden days, what you used to say was a simple "Clean your room." Two or three tries later, the work would get done. Since you had the hammer (allowance, car keys, etc.) back then, it was easy enough to obtain some level of compliance. Now you might wish to do something a little less adversarial. A conversation in which you point out that they are setting an example for their younger brothers and sisters, if there are still some in the house, is a start. Also, try to negotiate a compromise. For instance, maybe he won't clean the bedroom and make the bed every day, but he may agree to keep the door shut and to do the cleanup twice a week. If parents are flexible and rational, there is a 20 percent chance kids will return the favor.

Also, it's reasonable to insist that college students at home help with kitchen chores, yardwork, and laundry. Remind them that living as adults means they should be willing to take on some grown-up responsibilities. Most of the time it works better when you give them a task or chore, and then a zone of time in which to complete the project. For example, say, "I need the lawn mowed by Friday" on Tuesday. If your son or daughter is given ample warning before you expect the task to be completed, he or she may be willing to choose a time and do the deed. It's a much better approach than just saying, "Go out and mow the lawn, *now*," which you know will lead to a confrontation. In general, it's probably best to talk to them in a new language, one that is less autocratic and more cooperative.

Things like phone calls and visits from friends require special consideration. You can't keep being awakened by late-night phone calls. Coming and going is also disruptive. As a parent, you need to be firm and to insist that they show some level of courtesy and respect. If you don't, the cost will be much higher as your anger festers, leading to an eventual explosion. Ironing out small differences now is better than having shouting matches later.

If worse comes to worst, and it becomes apparent that your youngster simply is not willing to do his or her part, then you probably will need to pull out the heavy artillery. This includes telling them to move, cutting back on financial support, or taking action that you believe is fair, not vindictive, and that makes your point clear.

Holidays and summertimes can be stressful. Firm but sensible house rules, lots of dialogue, and the proper positioning of the moon can make it possible to survive. When it works right, parents can actually enjoy a returning student, at least for a time. The sailing won't necessarily be smooth, but the journey can be made.

14

Keeping in Contact

This time in history has been called the information age. The recent explosion of technological advances makes it possible to transmit data in ways most people never would have imagined. E-mail, the Internet, fax machines, overnight express mail, along with new telephone systems, create a multitude of methods for reaching out to people in faraway places.

Information, however, does not equal *communication*—as college parents are bound to discover. The old cliché, "out of sight, out of mind" applies well to the busy college undergrad. Family members are left to beg, coax, and tease even basic information from the new college student. Real communication is mostly just a dream.

Still, parents want to find out what's going on in their children's lives. Success in this aspect of managing the college experience requires parental cunning, creativity, and tenacious effort. It's important to succeed. Ignorance, in many circumstances, is not bliss. Not knowing can be disastrous.

The key to establishing productive contacts with college students is to have a game plan. It's also crucial to use communication skills such as effective listening, along with the ability to translate effectively, if you want to know what is going on with your kid while he or she attends college.

Communication Skills

The first step in creating your communication "game plan" is to figure out which parent is most "tuned in" to the youngster involved. Some dads have a hard time talking with sons, and some moms seem to regularly antagonize their daughters. Cross-gender conversations may work out better. In any case, be honest with yourselves. Identify which parent is most likely to achieve a meaningful dialogue with the young person in question. Take the quiz in Table 14.1. If you score low, maybe you're not the one.

TABLE 14.1

A Brief Quiz to See If You Live at Least Partly in Their World

1. Who sings the theme song to *Friends*?
2. Which group had a member die from a heroin overdose?
   (a) Stone Temple Pilots
   (b) Smashing Pumpkins
   (c) The Rolling Stones
   (d) all of the above
3. Who is the lead singer for Pearl Jam?
4. Who is Hootie? Coolio? Jenny McCarthy?
5. Which war do current college students remember best?
6. Who was president when most of today's college students were born?
7. Which show once featured Luke Perry?
   (a) *Baywatch*
   (b) *Beverly Hills 90210*
   (c) *My So-Called Life*
8. Who sang "All I Wanna Do Is Have Some Fun (on the Santa Monica Boulevard)"?
9. Whose name does the audience chant during commercials on *Late Night, With Conan O'Brian*?
10. Who was the babe in the movie *Clueless*?
11. What does "the bomb" mean?

(The answers are at the end of this chapter.)

Of course, learning a bunch of "young people trivia" is not really the secret to successful communication. Some parents just are better at getting their kids to open up and talk than others are. The main things to discover are the key details about their lives and their ongoing college experience. These include knowing:

- how many classes he's failing
- when boyfriend or girlfriend problems are affecting grades
- if she's dropping too many classes
- how their living arrangements are working out
- if your kid is having roommate problems
- which major he or she has chosen or changed to
- if he or she has health problems
- if he or she has serious psychological problems or is showing other troubling signals

Unfortunately, most sons are prone to grunts and one-word responses when asked about their lives. Most daughters give an "Oh, Mom" or "Oh, Dad" nonanswer when they think you're intruding too much into their personal situations. The persistent parent knows how to get past these comebacks and on to some real news without being too obvious.

Selecting a Medium

After choosing the main parental spokesperson, the next task is to select a means of communication. Many choices are available. One simple and new technique can be purchased just about anywhere. It's called a *phone card*. These prepaid cards make it possible for students to just pick up a phone and call home without putting in coins *or* calling collect. This costs more than other media, but it's worth the price, if that's the only way to get them to respond. Other options include:

E-mail. If you're on-line and have Internet access, kids can normally find a computer somewhere on campus to write to you directly. They may like this approach, because they get to fiddle with a computer. It's an easy, simple way to maintain contact, and the cost is low. Letters via this instrument tend to be short—but so what? At least you hear from them, and you know your mail get transmitted immediately. E-mail is also an excellent method of notify someone of an emergency, provided she reads her mail every day. Most colleges help students create E-mail accounts with convenient access.

Home 800 (not 900) number. Some parents (and students) prefer talking to writing. As with the phone card, there is some expense to a personalized 800 number, but, again, if they won't contact you any other way, this is a pretty good option. One major advantage of this medium is that you can talk whenever you want, for as long as you want, without incurring massive extra charges. Kids like this, because they are able to call from a regular in-room phone rather than a pay phone.

Fax. A few colleges offer fax services for students. It's expensive, letters tend to be short, and they aren't very private. Plus, a fax can get lost in a pile fairly easily.

Collect calls home. These are expensive and usually very short, because you're sitting there watching your watch throughout the call. Buy calling cards instead.

Have them call you, and pay them back. Many college dormitories and Greek houses have standard phone lines installed in individual rooms. For a regular monthly fee, your son or daughter has access to long-distance service. As a result, he or she can call more cheaply during low-rate periods (weekends, nights, etc.) and talk for longer periods of time. Prearranged times for calls to be made can be agreed upon. The major problem is that they'll blow the reimbursement money you send—before their phone bill arrives. Thus, they'll get behind on payments and eventually have their service cut off. Not only that, they'll forget all about the prearranged times to call, so you'll end up sitting home all night waiting for the phone to ring. As everyone knows, that feeling stinks.

Old-fashioned mail. Some high-tech types now call this "snail mail." Yep, it moves slowly, some people's handwriting is hard to decipher, and it's the easiest thing to put off for most kids. As parents, you can write to them fairly regularly and hope they pick up the habit. Some collegians find mail in the box to be a great morale booster and will respond to every letter. Others just don't bother.

Figure out which of these styles fits your kid, and choose the option that works best. Table 14.2 is a variation of snail mail. It's a *form letter*, which transmits at least some basic information. Xerox it and send a packet to school with your kid.

TABLE 14.2
College Form Letter

Dear: Mom   Dad   Mom & Dad
        (*please circle the appropriate choice*)

Hi there. I'm:

_____ fine
_____ bored
_____ frustrated and angry   (*check all that apply*)
_____ lonesome
_____ ready for a break
_____ tired
_____ happy

Because:

(a)   my classes are too easy
                    or   Answer: _____
(b)   my classes are too hard
                    and:
(a)   things are great with _____, my
      boyfriend/girlfriend
                    or   Answer: _____
(b)   _____, my boyfriend/girlfriend, and
      I just had a fight

How are you, Mom and Dad?

Answer: _____:

Circle the appropriate statement:

1. I have lots of friends on campus.
2. I have a few friends here.
3. I'm a lonely outcast.

1. My car is running great.
2. My car is running lousy.
3. My car is impounded because of my traffic tickets.
4. I just wrecked my car.

1. You can expect me home next holiday.
2. You can expect me home this weekend.
3. I'm not sure when I'll be home next.
4. I'm never coming home.

My activities are going well. Right now I'm:
(*check all that apply*)

_____ playing varsity sports, especially _____
_____ playing intramurals   (fill in the blank)
_____ cheerleading
_____ in the pep band
_____ studying instead of going to games
_____ playing lots of video games
_____ fighting to reinstate the Dalai Lama to his rightful position
_____ in several on-campus clubs, including _____
_____ in a play   (fill in the blank)
_____ in the chorus
_____ in the student government
_____ helping the local city government with its foreign policy
_____ writing for the school newspaper
_____ organizing an on-campus group to improve the social environment
_____ not doing anything
_____ thinking it's not wise to tell you what I've been doing

Please send money. _____ (*designate the amount*)
I need cash for: _____ books
                   _____ spending money
                   _____ a new one-time fee they're charging. Yeah, it's uh, for the uh, new sports arena, and uh, I need it before my court appearance, uh, I mean spring registration.

Love you lots,
_____, your   son   daughter (*circle one*)

As you can see, this handy, time-saving device may solve many communication problems. If you *really* want them to write, you also will have to provide envelopes, stamps, and probably a word processor of some sort.

No matter what the method, it's important to try to keep the lines of communication open. Your child should feel free to tell you about his or her problems and concerns, as well as triumphs and successes. Sometimes you'll be able to help, if in no other way than by being a good listener. When the tidings are good, parents deserve to share in the wins. After all, you're paying the tab, and you paid the dues all along to get your child to this point. Honestly, however, kids are kids, and you'll have to be quite diligent if you want to stay informed about your youngster's college career.

Casual Conversations

Most of the time, conversations with your youngster, by phone or in print, are going to be pretty banal. Exciting or dramatically depressing stuff doesn't happen every week. Consequently, short and pleasant conversations are best for the routine contacts. Many times it will be tough to find something to say. Think back to the time when you were that age. What kinds of words would have been most meaningful to you? Say them to your collegian. Here are some possibilities:

- "We are proud of you."
- "If you work hard, eventually good things will happen."
- "College seems like a long grind, but the payoffs are great."
- "You're setting a good example for your brothers and sisters."
- "Your grandparents are so pleased with how you're turning out."

Besides words of encouragement, think about things that would actually interest a college student. You know what they like. Ask about that. Relay local items of note. For example, they'll be glad to hear about their friends, especially the ones who are engaged, who are having babies, and who just got put in jail. Also, tell your kids where you saw their various acquaintances working. They'll probably be less interested in hearing about your job problems, your financial worries, and your view of the political scene. Use common sense in these routine chats. Remember, the best way to get most people to think you're smart and witty is to have them talk about themselves. So it is with college students.

The other major challenge in communicating with a college kid is translation. Many times what they say and what they mean are very different things. To know what's truly going on means paying attention, listening carefully, and drawing the proper conclusions. Table 14.3 is a guide to help you decode the meanings of their various utterances.

TABLE 14.3
Communications

What They Say	*What They Mean*
"I need money for tuition."	Actually, the tuition bill comes later, but you two seem pretty gullible.
"I need money for books."	I need book money plus a little for my slush fund.
"I need some money."	I don't really need money, but I want to maintain the exorbitant lifestyle to which I've become accustomed.
"I'm broke. Can you guys help out?"	I really do need a little money.
"Classes are going great!"	I'm passing all but one of my classes.
"I guess classes are okay."	I'm passing about half of my classes.
"I'm having problems in some of my classes."	If I pass one class, it will be a tremendous victory.
"I got in a little trouble in one class."	I got caught with crib notes, and they're considering academic suspension.

What They Say	*What They Mean*
"My teachers are okay."	My teachers have no idea who I am.
"My teachers are fun."	We have outdoor classes and watch lots of movies. Of course, we don't learn anything.
"The professor is a pain."	I actually have to work, and study for tests.
"The professor hates me."	He/she calls on me in class when I'm asleep.
"The professor really likes me."	It's the only class where I'm making an A.
"The food is good."	I eat out most of the time.
"The food is okay."	I use the meal service about twice a week.
"The food is terrible."	I'm eating out of vending machines in the student center.
"I went to a party last week. It was okay."	Had a few brews, told a few stories, went home early.
"I went to a party last week. I had a pretty good time."	I got pretty drunk, met a new man/woman. I got in about 4:00 A.M.
"I went to a party last week. I had a really good time."	"We did body shots. Several people were naked. I stayed up all night."
"I went to a party last week. We had a terrific time."	*You don't want to know.*
"My boyfriend/girlfriend is okay."	"We're thinking about seeing other people."
"My boyfriend/girlfriend is great."	"We're inseparable."
"My boyfriend/girlfriend says hi."	"We're thinking about marriage."

What They Say	*What They Mean*
"I need to talk to you."	Either "I'm pregnant" or "We just eloped."
"How's everyone at home?"	"I'm homesick."
"I miss you."	"It won't be long until I'm home for a visit."
"I can't stand it here."	*See below.*

As is evident, translation is a crucial issue when communicating with a college student. After you make contact, you can respond appropriately only if you know what is actually being said. Unfortunately, sometimes what kids say is extremely troubling. Constructing a reasoned response is every bit as difficult.

The Words You Don't Want to Hear

There are, in fact, many things you don't want to hear from your college student. Besides not wanting to find out that she is pregnant, drunk, or on drugs, there is one other phrase that sends chills down the spines of most parents of college kids: *"I'm thinking about dropping out."*

Makes you shiver, doesn't it? The ramifications of these five little words are enormous. They may mean any or all of the following:

- all that money you've spent so far may be going down the drain
- your hopes and dreams for their future are dying, or at best are on hold
- he or she is going to feel like a failure
- my child may be *moving back home*

Questions will quickly race through your mind. What will he do? Work? Transfer to another school? Buy a motorcycle and tour the country? Is it because she wants to get married? Is she pregnant? Is she just trying to get even? *What are we going to do?*

Your peaceful home is going to be changed again. You need a strategy, a response. Here are some tactics:

Find out why.　Don't by angry or judgmental. Just be persistent until you get the truth. Maybe your youngster had a bad day and merely needed to vent. It could be that the decision is well-reasoned and has been a long time in coming. Parents can't react correctly unless they know whether their child's desire to leave school is based on reason, emotion, idle whim, or something else.

Tell them your feelings.   It's fair to say you're disappointed. It's reasonable to convey how upsetting the announcement is for both parents. Even expressing anger is probably better than bottling it up and blasting him or her later. A few parents may even say they are relieved or not surprised. They may have suspected all along that this college was the wrong place, or that university life in general probably wasn't going to work out. In any case, you're an adult and they're becoming adults. Tell them the truth about what you are thinking and feeling.

Develop a strategy.   There are a series of options available to the potential dropout. They include:

- immediate withdrawal from school (which is best if he or she has major personal problems, and coping with any more would be counterproductive)
- finish the semester (which is best if the student can pass many or most classes without major damage to a grade point average)
- taking a semester off (working for a few months at some menial job may convince him that college is the better option)
- counseling (colleges provide people—psychologists, student advisers, and even peer counselors—who specialize in student moral issues)
- transferring (maybe your son or daughter needs a less rigorous curriculum, more individualized attention, or a less challenging city to live in)
- providing diversions (sometimes loneliness drives a student to decide to drop out; encourage your student to try new activities. He or she could audition for a play or help build scenery, join a club in his or her major, or take up a new hobby. Simple involvement might make a big difference)

Take a deep breath.   Keep in mind that you don't have to solve the problem in one day. Any course of action will take some time. Careful, measured actions are better than frantic and panicked reactions. A calm demeanor may rub off on the troubled college student, allowing both of your to face the situation more rationally.

Remember what you learned in chapter 5: The choice of a college (or a major, or a roommate, or most things, when you think about it) is not engraved in stone. People change, they make mistakes, and they decide it's time to try something new. Part of being an adult, and helping your youngster feel more grown up, is recognizing when a hopeless situation requires an actual change. In contrast, your kid needs to learn how to distinguish a hopeless situation from merely difficult circumstances.

Go with the flow. Once a resolution has been reached, parents should understand how the lives of everyone involved will be in flux for a time. The former student may move home or in with friends. He or she may seem depressed and defeated, or the new dropout may feel energized by not having to cope with what had become impossible conditions.

As a parent, your task is to keep your youngster from dwelling on the past. What is crucial is deciding what venture to pursue next. Believe it or not, some students will quickly reverse their course and go right back to the same college or university they left. Others will go to work for a time. Some will transfer to a new school. The major goal for parents is to get them out of the house and involved in something new, as soon as possible. If you don't, your lives can quickly become like that of the old Middle Eastern shepherd who let his camel start putting its nose in the tent. (Those who don't know this story should read up on their fables. This one speaks particularly well to new college parents.)

Tough Topic Number One: Transfers

Communication is crucial in the case of transfers from one university to another. As parents, you need to know why your son or daughter believes the other college will be better than the current choice. Students shouldn't transfer because of:

1. Romance.   This ends, and then your child will really feel foolish.

2. Paranoia.   If they think a particular school or prof is out to get them, they'll soon feel the same way at the next place.

3. Friendships.   As noted earlier, high school relationships change once students go to college. A school choice should reflect a match of the student with a chosen major, a preferred lifestyle, and the student's academic skills. Friends can be made anywhere, especially at their age.

Talking the student through the transfer process takes patience. He or she will need to understand a few things. First, this setback really is a setback. Transfer students lose credits, since many schools will not accept every course from the previous college. Also, each college has an individualized set of core requirements (general ed classes), and it's likely your youngster will have to make up a few of these classes.

Second, moving is traumatic, and transferring students may move more than once. They often come home for a time and then move again to a new place. This means identifying key hangouts, such as gas stations, fast-food places, bars, and special-interest venues. Moving is hard for people of all ages. Combining moving with a new college setting doubles the stress level.

Third, a new version of homesickness is likely to evolve. Your son or daughter may be homesick for your house, as well as for the previous campus. Adjusting to new surroundings is never easy, and it makes the grass seem greener where they used to be.

It takes an empathetic parent to help a twenty-year-old cope with a transfer. Don't prosecute or blame. Don't say "I told you so" about their first choice (even if you were right). It's important to proclaim continuing support for his or her college career, even knowing that graduation is now farther down the road and that the costs have just risen as a result. Kids often feel they have failed when they change schools. It's your job to point out the value of a second chance. Encourage them to make the best of the new setting rather than dwelling on what caused them to leave the old one. After all, they're still trying. They still want to graduate. Most important, *they're still not living at home!*

Tough Topic Number Two: Substance Abuse

Another area of concern for parents trying to communicate with kids is substance abuse. Problems with alcohol as well as with drugs can turn a bright and promising college student into a burnt-out has-been in short order. No young man or woman who has this problem is likely to even consider discussing it with his or her parents.

Mom and Dad battle a tough foe when mind-altering substances are at issue. The adversary is *peer pressure.* Their so-called friends will entice them into chronic drinking and other bad habits. The best you can hope for is that your long-standing message has already sunk in. Kids now have access to drugs as early as grade school. By the time the college years roll around, seeing drug use is part of their daily lives.

It may be too much to expect to think they won't even experiment with marijuana or something stronger. Instead, be realistic. Your best strategy may be to let them know you are aware there are pleasant sensations associated with certain chemicals (otherwise, why would anyone use them?). On the other hand, strongly note what takes place later, the *aftereffects*—hangovers and addictions. Druggies and drunks are people who end up giving away their place in line. Achievements, recognition, and long-term success go to those who avoid these problems. There are serious consequences to substance abuse, and it's a world full of temptation.

When you get a strong sense that your son or daughter has an alcohol or drug problem, you should contact the school's counseling center or dean of students. Until your son or daughter recognizes that he or she has a problem, there won't be a whole lot you can do. If he or she finally does ask for help, contact Alcoholics Anonymous, or the nearest community mental health center to get your child in touch with the right people. You may wish to visit an Al-Anon or a Narcotics Anonymous (Nar-Anon) program for emotional support.

Tough Topic Number Three: Gambling

Nearly 25 percent of today's college students gamble. It's all around them, with lotteries, racetracks, riverboat gambling, casinos, and readily accessible gambling cities. Today's kids have grown up with gambling in everyday life. At most universities there is well-established illegal gambling activity, (through bookies and numbers runners). This issue is one that should demand your attention. Gambling is addictive and dangerous. If your son or daughter even jokes about betting on a sporting event, take it seriously. Try to have a heart-to-heart talk about how quickly a few casual bets can turn into a big problem. As with smoking, it's much easier to never start than to try to quit.

Tough Topic Number Four: Credit Cards

Many banks and financial institutions want to train your youngster in concert with the college. What these folks teach young people is how to bury themselves in plastic right away and spend the rest of their lives trying to get out from under. The lure of a credit card is overwhelming for most eighteen- to twenty-two-year-olds. It means they are being treated more like adults, and that they have access to money even when there isn't any in the bank. Having a credit card becomes a status symbol to many young adults.

Unfortunately for parents, credit cards can mean that their kid is about to become swamped with debt. Many teenagers and people in their early twenties simply aren't very good at things like budgeting and managing money. For some, using a card makes them feel as if their purchases don't cost anything. Even more savvy kids are likely to forget to account for interest payments when they suppose they will be able to take care of the bill.

Warnings and dire predictions of financial ruin are your best approach. Simply tell your kid you want him to have nothing to do with credit cards, unless he can somehow convince you he can handle it. Tell her that if she gets a card she should only use it for *real* emergencies. You should be prepared, however, for the possibility that they will completely ignore your advice and make a big mess of things anyway! Banks are counting on them to do just that.

Once your kid is overwhelmed with debt, make a deal. Cut up the card in exchange for helping with payments. Use the leverage you have (your checkbook) to help work your way through this dilemma. Although credit limits on college cards are fairly low, they are still high enough to be truly troublesome to Mom and Dad, especially when they have to bail out their debt-ridden kid.

In general, keeping in contact with a college student is both an art and a science. It's a science in the sense that parents must recognize how many factors, including age or the mere mention of grades, will change conversational patterns. It's an art to translate what they are trying to tell you. It's both because new experiences, brushes with influential professors, and peer pressures from friends, not to mention significant others, will change how your child talks to you. The language will be different, the outlook altered, and the means of expression changed. Maybe you were used to your son or daughter communicating through tantrums when at home. It's possible, however, that he or she will grow up enough to be able to converse rather than scream. To help this process along, you must both be watchful to not fall into old habits. Avoid escalating old, unwinnable arguments. Seek topics everyone will enjoy discussing. Many times you can actually talk about the content of their classes—authors they enjoyed, subjects they liked—instead of debating whether or not they are required to make their beds every day. Be encouraging, positive, unpretentious, open, and try to assist their transformation into adults. What you make of this time will determine how interactions proceed for the next several years. Let them grow up. Both of you will benefit.

Many avenues are available to let them know you still love them and are concerned with their well-being. For example, many colleges, or businesses near campus, offer what are essentially "care packages" for various times during the year. If not, put together one on your own. The new school semester can be met with a package of razors, soaps, shampoos, tissues, and so forth. The week of the finals can be made easier with a package of snack foods, coffee, a pick-me-up note, flowers, and other morale boosters. Small, "I'm-thinking-of-you" cards and letters, which don't require a response, can let them know they're in your thoughts. Not all communication takes place through words. Parents who take the time to keep in touch offer encouragement and show concern are the ones who will get visits in their old age from grateful and caring kids. All relationships require the investment of time and energy to keep them working.

Therefore, for goodness' sake, don't ever make the mistake of leaving your kid to call your voice mail or talk to your answering machine. If you depersonalize communication now, it may stay that way forever!

Answers to Table 14.1

1. The Rembrandts
2. b, Smashing Pumpkins (if you said the Rolling Stones, you're too far gone)
3. Eddie Vedder
4. Lead singer of Hootie and the Blowfish; rapper; hot blonde featured in "Singled Out" on MTV
5. The Gulf War
6. Gerald Ford or Jimmy Carter (Reagan is coming up soon)
7. b, *Beverly Hills 90210*
8. Cheryl Crow
9. Andy, Andy, Andy
10. Alicia Silverstone
11. Very cool

15

As Time Passes

High-quality parents of college kids are like lighthouses. They stand on the shoreline, weathering the storm, brightly pointing the way. Unfortunately, college students are often like yellow submarines with the periscope turned backward. Rest assured, however, that as time passes college kids tend to straighten themselves out and start navigating more effectively. When this finally happens, two phenomena occur. First, they notice the light from the tower and occasionally make use of the guidance it provides. Second, they begin to appreciate the fact that the lighthouse is there, and has been there, all this time.

In other words, once your son or daughter gets through the freshman year, it's often possible to take some comfort in what you see. For instance, you begin to sense that, more likely than not, since he has passed four to eight (or more) classes, he is capable of finishing school. Also, you begin to believe she is capable of living away from home, at least part of the time. There still may be some false starts when they change majors (chapter 12) or when they transfer (chapter 14), but soon the tide will turn in your favor.

The typical, traditional-age college student, who enrolls right after high school and pursues a regular four- or five-year degree program, goes through a series of predictable phases. College professors and others watch the evolution, year in and year out. You only see it every once in a while. As a result, some preparation concerning the various mutations they display over the years might help you work with them toward the eventual goal: graduation, getting a job, and freedom for your wallet! Table 15.1 summarizes a few of the changes you will notice.

TABLE 15.1
Key Characteristics, By Class

Freshmen	Sophomores	Juniors	Seniors	
			(1st semester)	(2nd semester)
wide-eyed	confident	cocky	unbearable	shaken confidence
shy/retiring	blooming	pushy	arrogant	cautious
enthusiastic	calm	casual	bored	reawakened
confused	in control	egocentric	obnoxious	self-analytical
anxious	relaxed	sleepy	comatose	anxious
lonely	friendly	macho (male) diva (female)	hip socialite	insecure insecure
homesick	home for weekends/ holidays	home for holidays	home for money	rarely home

As previously noted, freshmen are shy and retiring sorts in many social settings. They go through many of the emotions described in chapter 7. Attrition rates (dropouts, transfers) are highest in the freshman class. College administrators continually work on programs designed to reduce attrition rates. One thing they have learned is that what attracts a student to a college is not what keeps that person on board. Students tend to *choose* colleges based on parental wishes, beauty of the campus, availability of scholarships and loans, friendliness of the recruiter, and location. What *keeps* a kid on campus includes friends, interactions with college professors, subjects of interest, campus activities, and romance.

Consequently, the business of recruiting students is different from the task of keeping them. College leaders do their best to retain students. They offer tutoring, mentoring, counseling, and other hug 'em and love 'em activities, and, as discussed in chapter 7, require freshman orientation classes. Do not, for an instant, believe that such classes are offered with some philanthropic purpose in mind. No, the administration is not trying to help you out. What they are interested in is keeping your money—and if it is a state-supported school, the government's money.

Most state-supported colleges receive governmental funding based on the number of students in school or the hours of credit taught. That's because most of them only generate about 20 to 40 percent of their revenues from tuition. The rest comes from state government and federal funds, which are based on what are known as *head counts* of individuals enrolled.

Therefore, colleges need students. That's why they spend vast amounts of time and money on recruiting, which you may have noticed from the brochures, letters, and other junk mail you began receiving around your child's fifteenth birthday. All those potential students are quickly sorted down to the few who actually enroll at a particular school. It does the college very little good to get a bunch of high school seniors to sign on and then flunk them out as freshmen! In addition, each individual department on campus receives budgetary amounts based on credit hours and students. So they, too, have a strong desire to keep your kid around.

As a result, parents can expect the most help from the university during the first year of school. Administrators know they retain a greater percentage of each class (more sophomores than freshmen, more juniors than sophomores, etc., as a college career continues. You can dovetail their efforts with yours by following all of the sage advice provided in this book, up to this point. After that, each year presents new challenges and difficulties. Careful analysis of these changes can help you cope with the entirety of the college career.

Sophomores

There is a glimmer of confidence in a sophomore's eye. Be glad it's there. Only in sports is there truly a "sophomore jinx." In academics, students are better prepared for the rigors of school, the routine of study, the pressure of tests, and other demands of college life.

The one temptation luring sophomores, which may invite parental intervention, is in the area of constructing a schedule. Kids at about this age tend to want to take a set of easy classes—there are affectionate nicknames for these (e.g. "pud class"), which vary from school to school—in order to accommodate their blossoming social calendars. This means they'll line up twelve hours (four classes) instead of fifteen (five), and none of the courses will be very demanding. You need to point out that too much goofing around now is going to make the senior year pretty intense. Try to keep them on a reasonable track toward graduation without seeming like you're trying to boss them around.

One other issue parents may encounter concerns the actual courses they're taking. Your son or daughter will happily be completing general ed classes, and moving on to classes related to a major or minor. If he or she is still undecided about a major, a certain amount of concern will start to develop. Don't add to their anxiety by leaning on them too much. It will happen when the time is right. Encourage them to experiment in special-interest courses. These fill the *elective* part (nongeneral education and nonmajor classes) of a college program, and may help him or her decide upon which major to select. Most college programs allow for twelve to twenty hours of general purpose electives. The sophomore year is a good time to use them, especially when the student has not declared or decided on a major.

Socially, sophomores tend to get off campus more and venture out into the town or city. A key factor here is the drinking age. Most states require adults to be twenty-one years old to enter a tavern. Sophomores are about twenty years old. Consequently, fake IDs become more valuable than gold. Parents can meet the inevitable arrest with one of three responses:

1. If you wanna dance, you gotta pay the band.
2. We were young once and did equally stupid things.
3. We're going to help, but you're going to pay us back and promise not to do it again.

The chosen response depends on parental views and values, of course. It should also hinge on whether or not your son or daughter was *driving* under the influence. Since the student is gone from home, Mothers Against Drunk Drivers (MADD) contracts (in which the child agrees to call home when inebriated and the parent agrees to pick the child up, no questions asked) don't work. Still, each parent should consider it to be a critical duty to solicit an ironclad agreement from the child concerning drinking and driving. Remind him or her that there are other options, such as designated drivers, cab services, and walking! Someone's life could be at stake.

One other major area that parents sometimes wish to influence is romance. Typically, a high school sweetheart is discarded by the sophomore year of college. At that point, some students immediately tie themselves down to someone new instead of playing the field. Mom and Dad ultimately have little say in this aspect of their kid's private life. Still, you might try suggesting the value of having a group of close friends, rather than one single romantic partner.

Many students form close relationships with companions who can make the whole college experience run more smoothly. One friend may serve as a study buddy, another as confidant, and so forth. Encourage your son or daughter not to depend on one person to meet all needs. Of course, you can't just come out and give directions. Instead, describe how a circle of friends and acquaintances broadened the scope of your youthful experiences. Make a case that a clan is better than just one person. Provide examples of kids they know who limited their future options by being romantically and emotionally tied down. In other words, get the idea across: *There is no hurry to find one mate!*

Some kids will actually find this advice to be a relief! Serving the wishes of one romantic partner is time-consuming and limiting. Clearly there are instances where love is real and best for both partners but, in others, love is less mature than it will some day become. Hope that your son or daughter can tell the difference.

There can be a tragic side to college dating. Date rape reports reach their highest levels during the college years. Make sure you have given your kids all the appropriate words of caution that you can. Fraternities, sororities, and school counselors can also help. Student escort services for night classes, planned activities, campus lighting, and other preventive measures should be in place at the school. Having a game plan is crucial—encourage your kid to develop one. Being forewarned may keep your daughter less susceptible to such an attack and keep your son aware of the line between seduction and coercion. It's wise to remind kids of both genders that alcohol is often a major factor in instances of date rape.

Meanwhile, you'll notice that communication is a little more difficult in the sophomore year. That's because they call less often, write less frequently, and aren't as inclined to come home. Their old high school friends are off doing new things. College friends will keep them on campus more weekends. Also, if they become active in college clubs, bands, or intramurals, they'll want to be around to take part in their activities. Consequently, parents will need to take greater initiative to keep the lines of communication open. At the same time, the student is likely to be less open, if not secretive, about what he or she has been doing. Reread chapter 14 regarding keeping in contact, and put more effort into understanding the college student's world.

Somewhere between the sophomore and junior year of school will occur one of the most common college experiences: taking part in a fad, fashion, or fixation. Nearly every student is influenced by these trends. Some fads are just for fun, while others are political statements. Take a look at Table 15.2, which lists crazes of previous years. Expect your youngster to get involved in some new variation that comes along, and don't be a stick-in-the-mud about it.

Sophomores are a mix of new confidence and old insecurity. Parents should seek out ways to bolster the student's confidence and methods to allay insecurities. This isn't the same old high school kid being dethroned by college. The sophomore year is the time of transition from a timid and quiet kid to an annoying and overbearing junior. So enjoy it for what it's worth. It won't be long until the freshman and sophomore years will seem like the good old days.

TABLE 15.2
Campus Activities and Fads (1950s–1990s)

panty raids	poodle skirts with big hair
toga parties	letter sweaters
sit-ins	no makeup
love-ins	long hair/sideburns
streaking	tie-dyed everything
disco parties	bell bottoms, balloon sleeves, backless dresses, platform shoes
The "Assassin" game	*Miami Vice* look (unshaven, Italian deck shoes, no socks, three-quarter-sleeve coat)
retro parties/sock hops	Madonna look (bustier, leather)
grunge	homeless look
macarena	tattoos, earrings in unusual places, sandals and socks

Juniors

Is there anything worse than a junior in college? Philosophers and professors have posed this question for nearly a millennium. What you have is a twenty- to twenty-one-year-old person, filled with hormones, fired by alcohol, invigorated by some level of academic success, inspired by friends, coddled by lovers, and taught by pompous professors. Naturally, such an individual is brimming with the arrogance of overconfidence. Once again, this know-it-all who wonders how you ever got this far in life will be a stranger to you. If one word could describe the typical junior, it would be: *smug*.

Expect to be bombarded by their political views. Their level of social consciousness will be at an all-time high. Most people will engage in more partisan activities in college than at any other point in their lives. They'll want to sucker you into the discourse, trying to persuade you with the wisdom of their newly discovered opinions (see Table 15.3). They couldn't be any more full of themselves.

TABLE 15.3
Things College Juniors Want to Talk About

- how to save the whales
- how to save the rain forests
- why mom and dad should recycle more, start a compost heap, and stop buying goods from corporate polluters
- why the corrupt political system is Dad's fault
- how college football players are barbarians, and why they shouldn't be allowed on campus
- why neo-Marxism is better than capitalism
- how greed is ruining society
- in general, how parents are responsible for all of the world's problems
- for *women:* how men are emotionally primitive and are nothing but narcissistic cretins
- for *men:* how women continually seek to emotionally castrate men for their own ego gratification
- for *both:* why you should give them a car for a graduation present next year (showing they've learned how to plan ahead)

Fun discussions, no? Meanwhile, against this backdrop, you are going to be trying to have reasonable and sensible conversations regarding more salient issues. You'll want to know if they've chosen a major—or if they're sticking with the one they selected. They won't want to tell you. Students at this age they truly resent being told what to do about anything. They want to arrange their own schedules, pick their own classes, and, in general, manage their own lives. Except, of course, they still want you to pick up the tab.

College juniors tend to know the system well enough to figure out how to graduate on time. Most universities have some sort of advisory system, whereby the student can sit down and finalize an approach to finishing school. Half of the junior class takes advantage of this offer. The other half forges their advisor's name on all documents. The latter group ordinarily finds out they've missed one or two classes and won't be done by May of the senior year. Go ahead, let them fix their own problems at this point. They have to learn, sooner or later.

Socially, juniors are rowdy, aggressive, and basically out of control. Be glad they're on campus. They don't come home much, except to ask for money and favors. Most have a solid set of friends to get into trouble with on a routine basis. Many have settled on a boyfriend or girlfriend. Couples events, such as double dates, are common. Your son or daughter will be extremely noncommittal when you ask about romance. If they're headed toward the altar, they don't want you to know just yet. If they're just messing around, well, they figure it's none of your business. And truthfully, maybe it isn't. Recall your own love life at that age. Give your son or daughter some space.

If there is ever a time to keep them on campus during spring break or summer, it's the junior year. Who needs a cocky so-and-so pointing out your flaws during the warmest months of the year, when tempers are already short? Besides, their expanding social life is getting expensive. Encourage them to work on campus during the school year and somewhere else the rest of the time.

A serene home life often characterizes the year for parents of college juniors. Visits from kids aren't likely, save for mandatory holiday appearances. They won't be in contact much. When they do come around, you're still not going to receive much information about their activities. As a result, parents should mainly make sure no one is pregnant, grades are okay, and no lawsuits are pending.

In many ways the junior year is an interesting time. A youngster finishing general ed classes and starting with entry-level courses in a given major will probably be most pleased with how things are going in the classroom. You should feel one form of relief, since academics won't be a problem area, unless the wrong major was chosen or the kid simply isn't trying. Unfortunately, parents are often left in the dark concerning most aspects of school. Perhaps that's okay, however, because this year starts what will become a major transition into adulthood. Let them have their fun for now. Life will get even with them soon enough.

Seniors

The senior year begins as a continuation of the junior year. That is, first semester seniors are brimming with overconfidence and have become extremely easygoing about college life. They know the ropes. They're kings of the hill once again. Most have good friends, involvements on campus, favorite professors, plus enjoyable clubs and groups to which they belong. They have all of their favorite hangouts figured out, for lunch, dinner, weekends, holidays, dates, and everything in between.

For the majority of college students, part of the senior year is a kind of last hurrah—last homecoming, last Thanksgiving trip home, and one final Christmas break. Students try to enjoy this time, buckling down, making better grades, and feeling better about themselves as a result. They see the light at the end of the tunnel. They are about to conquer the mountain. A quiet sense of confidence and even serenity emerges. At this stage, friends, familiarity, and fun rule the day.

In high school, those about to graduate develop symptoms of *senioritis*. These included inattentiveness, laziness, and a general lack of interest in school. The only goal was to get it over with. College seniors also have a common set of tendencies, which are displayed in Table 15.4.

TABLE 15.4
Symptoms of Collegiate Senioritis

- a highly refined ability to skip class
- for males, carefully crafted tactics for admiring the ladies
- for females, skillfully polished methods of flirting, even when one's boyfriend is standing nearby
- mastery at putting down freshmen and others whom they disdain (dormies, Greeks, geeks, etc.)
- state-of-the-art "cramming" capabilities

- adeptness in writing term papers overnight
- restless feeling that they should be making more money
- well-developed techniques for getting money out of Mom and Dad

---

As parents, you are familiar with the routine of paying tuition bills, know how much money to expect to dole out each month, and know when to expect your kids to come around. You're veterans of the Parents Day scene and probably have skipped at least one by now. Home life for parents is settled. After various visits over the years, you are used to the disruptions they cause, and you probably have discovered your own ways to get through them.

This final holding pattern can't last forever, for you or for your child. A new crisis is about to emerge. Somewhere during the first few months of the senior season, it dawns on your child that life beyond the campus is soon going to be an unavoidable reality. At that instant he or she will take one of two routes. A large percentage of seniors score the highest grades of their college careers during the first semester. They work harder, study more, party less, and generally take school more seriously. The others just give up. They know their grades are disastrous, so they just play out the string, trying to make it through by the skin of their teeth. Mom and Dad should profoundly hope their child fits into the first category. By now, there isn't much else you can do.

Soon, parents will be startled to hear questions about careers, job applications, and other aspects of the *real world*. A few will even ask about graduate school. This stage in a college career represents an opportunity. Some real bonding can transpire when you sit down with your son or daughter and discuss options for the future in detail. What you will be watching is the most adult form of dethronement most people encounter. As opposed to other de-thronement experiences, this time the kid *knows* he or she is about to get dumped back down to the bottom rung. Being a willing and helpful mentor creates significant new links that improve and deepen your relationship with your youngster. Remember, they're going to start showing signs of vulnerability soon, so treat them carefully. Don't assume they have everything under control. Being a concerned listener is as helpful as anything else you can do.

Arriving at the midpoint of senior year is comparable to having a bucketful of cold water dumped on you on a hot summer day. This chilling experience awakens the most placid senior. Soon every single aspect of existence is shaken to the foundation. Consider what changes after graduation:

- where they live
- what they do
- where their friends live
- how they get money
- how they spend weekends
- drinking/dating partners

In short, seniors quickly become acutely aware of how much life is about to be altered. For the first time in a long time, parents will see hints of insecurity creeping back into their demeanor. What happens next is equally unsettling.

Senior Syndrome

Any time the world shifts dramatically, people in it grasp and grab for any assurance they can find. One major source of this type of support is a boyfriend or girlfriend. Hence, a substantial number of college seniors become engaged! Is this bad, good, or normal? It's hard to say. There is considerable evidence suggesting that many of these proposals of marriage emerge in part from fears about the future. People cling to whatever they can from college, and a romantic partner is an obvious starting point.

Counseling your youngster on the pros and cons of marriage, particularly at this unstable stage, is the subject for a whole other book. For now, your job is simply to be aware of what might be happening. One tactic to use in preparing for senior syndrome is to simply tell your child it might occur, before the school years begins. Avoid using an accusing or judgmental tone. State it matter-of-factly, such as "Well, I guess you'll be thinking about getting married soon. A lot of seniors do." Let that opener start the dialogue. This is one time when you can appear to be wise and knowledgeable. Your youngster may even be impressed that you know about the subject at all. Be honest with him or her. Tell him or her what you truly believe is the best option—matrimony, a holding pattern, or moving on.

Regression

A second form of reaction to senior insecurity is reverting to an earlier stage of development. Some college seniors may appear to become less mature than they were before. They'll want to move home, sleep in their old beds, and, in general, become emotionally dependent on Mom and Dad, for old times' sake. Others will overidealize their college experiences. They will cling to every second, continually talking about how they dread losing out on all the fun. The college offers one solution for these kids. *They turn them into freshman recruiters!* This isn't such a bad idea for some. It makes letting go over time just a little easier.

What you are witnessing during the final nine months of school is the last and most traumatic collegiate transition. What looms on the horizon is job-hunting, graduating, and leaving everything familiar. Colleges seek to help by putting on job fairs, instructing strudents in résumé preparation, and setting up on-campus interviews with numerous employers.

In case you've forgotten, going through the meat-market procedure of finding a job is one of the most demeaning experiences people endure. Seniors are especially vulnerable, since they must leave behind the familiarity of being students, which is the life they're lived for the past twelve to eighteen years, and enter a brand-new world. Lost confidence, fear, uneasiness, and many other similar emotions are likely.

As parents, relaying stories of your own past job searches may help. Misery *does* love company. Some folks may be able to assist their youngsters by facilitating contacts with potential employers. Anything you can do to make getting a job easier will be helpful. Let them know you're not expecting them to find some kind of lifelong employment commitment. Also, expect to be required to provide some transitional funding through the summer or until they finally get hired.

Many kids, especially liberal arts majors (English, Art, History, Drama, Speech Communication, etc.), may take things very seriously at this point. They'll be asking questions not only about what job to take, but what *career* to enter. They'll wonder about having a life and an identity in the real world. Parents mostly need to help them relax. Remind them that their primary chore should be to simply secure a job in an area that is comfortable, and let things develop from there. Tell them most college graduates change employers at least twice in the first five years after receiving a degree, and that, as a result, there is no reason for some big-time trauma.

Graduate School

A handful of seniors will begin to contemplate graduate school. For some, graduate school is a means to avoid entering the workforce, or is a last choice when all else has failed. For others, the process of moving on to grad school is by design. These students knew from the start that a four-year degree was only the beginning. Graduate school is a prerequisite for most careers in medicine, law, some areas of education and social work, the sciences, theology, and economics.

As a parent, help your son or daughter think through the decision to immediately head off to a graduate school. First of all, most people in their early twenties should think about taking a summer, a semester, or even a full year off before continuing the educational process. Earning a four-year bachelor's degree is a life-altering experience. It takes a while to totally absorb everything. Working for a time and earning spending money (plus cash for graduate school) is often advisable. Only the most intense, serious, motivated student should go straight on into a master's program or other graduate school.

Second, make certain your senior considers carefully which grad program to enter. This choice is more significant than the selection of an undergraduate institution. You don't want false starts and changes of programs at this level. Also, seeking the most prestigious school that is attainable is the best strategy.

In general, graduate studies are much tougher than bachelor's programs. Make certain your youngster is emotionally ready to take this next step. Instead of filling out job applications, the chore will be to sign up for graduate entrance exams, such as the Graduate Record Examination (GRE), the Graduate Management Admissions Test (GMAT), the Law School Admission Test (LSAT), etc. and send in applications to various academic institutions. Many students also apply for graduate-assistant positions and other forms of on-campus employment. Parents may be called upon to help their kids fill out all the graduate school paperwork. Consider it a privilege, because your youngster is seeking to take the next step and become a professional.

For most students, the second semester of the senior year is when most of their concerns will flare up. It requires a quick adjustment by parents, who must revert once again to supportive and empathetic roles. Meanwhile, toward the middle of the second semester will come the swan song spring break. If there is any way possible, try to let that last spring break be something to remember. Once the graduate starts a new job, vacations will be scarce, since he or she won't have the time nor the money to do much for several years.

Parents grow and change as much as students during the four years of college. The relationship between Mom and Dad, son and daughter, gets transformed, adapted, adjusted, and refined. To be a truly effective parent of a college student means rolling with the punches as the four years of school pass by. Soon enough graduation arrives and the final era of college parenting begins. Be happy you survived to this point.

16

Graduation Day

At long last, the day arrives. What seems like just a few short moments ago you were saying good-bye to a frightened freshman. Now, without so much as a time out, you must brace yourself for the big ceremony. Two thoughts will run through your mind simultaneously as you anticipate this event:

1. *I have been waiting for this day for an eternity!*
2. *How did it get here so fast?*

They've changed so much. You've aged so much. Wow, the clock is ticking! These are the thoughts that usually accompany the final major trial of college parenting: watching them graduate. Most folks experience a mixture of relief and regret as the time draws close. Although this final chapter can help you get ready, no amount of preparation can truly help you through this episode.

To begin with, graduation may seem much like the recruiting trips and other visits you've been making for the past several years. That is, the parental experience of this day is vastly different from what the child undergoes. Table 16.1 is a schedule of events for the big festival.

There are some variations on this format. For example, larger universities may have one overall "starter" ceremony, and then send everyone off to separate settings where individual diplomas are

TABLE 16.1
A Typical Graduation Day Schedule

8:00–9:00 A.M.	officer ceremony for ROTC students
9:00–10:00 A.M.	pinning ceremony for nurses
10:00–11:00 A.M.	president's reception for major brown-nosers and social climbers
11:00–12:00 noon	wander aimlessly
12:00 noon–1:00 P.M.	lunch (just *try* to find a cafe with an empty table)
1:00–1:25 P.M.	graduation procession
1:30 P.M.	everybody is actually seated
1:30 –2:00 P.M.	awarding of honorary degrees, distinguished alumni awards, and all that other junk no one cares about
2:00–2:30 P.M.	president's speech (students start getting restless)
2:30–3:00 P.M.	keynote speech (students consider violent rebellion)
3:00 P.M.	awarding of degrees (everyone is glad to get up and stretch)
3:05 P.M.	parents discover they forgot to buy film
4:00 P.M.	last diploma awarded (students look stunned and bored)
4:05 P.M.	bathrooms are flooded with ceremony participants
4:15–5:00 P.M.	students are reunited with parents and family (major photo opportunity)
5:30 P.M.	dinner (just *try* to find a resturant with an empty table)
6:30 P.M.	kids shuffle around, hinting that they're ready for Mom and Dad to leave
7:00 P.M.	Mom and Dad finally get the hint and leave

awarded. Normally schools or colleges within the university hold these separate rituals. Other colleges divide into halves, with one group graduating Friday night and the other on Saturday afternoon.

Also, the actual presentation is changed when the university confers graduate degrees. In these, each individual recipient is *cowled,* meaning that a hood or some other form of ornamental dress is individually draped over his or her shoulders. This takes time, boring the dickens out of everyone else.

Some institutions have so many graduates that identities are not conveyed as individuals cross the stage. For example, at the University of Nebraska the names of all new doctors (Ph.D., M.D., etc.) are recited, along with those of students receiving master's degrees, while undergraduates are funneled toward the front of the auditorium two-by-two, as if headed toward Noah's Ark, with only background music to serenade them as they make the trip. This can be a real bummer for parents who just spent four years and their life savings waiting for this moment.

Finally, a number of colleges have more than one graduation ceremony per year. A *mid-term* event is held in December or January, and one may be held at the close of summer school in August. These scaled-down commemorations are more intimate, and in some ways more enjoyable as a result. They don't feature the degree of delirium that surrounds the traditional May commencement.

Regardless of the structure of the days program, what you should expect is thirty seconds of excitement packed into a three-hour ceremony. Expect to sweat, because it's springtime for most graduations. Expect to be annoyed, because graduation days are scheduled and directed by college administrators. By now you should know what that entails, so do your best to make the event as pleasant as possible. To succeed, it's important to first understand what your child is experiencing.

The Graduate's Day

Soon-to-be graduates pay considerable attention to the list of people who will receive invitations to their graduation celebration. They will want to include their favorite people in conjunction with those most likely to give them expensive gifts. Invitations are sold to students during the spring of the senior year (usually through the college bookstore), and naturally become one more cost for parents to bear as part of the process. Expect a small confrontation over how many to order and mail. You'll want to pare the list down; the graduate will want to expand it to every potential member of the gift-giving pool. At the same time, students should be aware that some schools actually limit the number of people who can attend the graduation ceremony. Thus, a balance must be achieved between invitations sent only to collect gifts and those sent to actually ask people to attend the ceremony.

For the most part, graduation ceremony attendees will include parents, family (especially grandparents and siblings), friends, and any significant other of note. It takes some thought and effort to coordinate logistics for a group this large. Remember, restaurants will be jammed, hotels will be booked, traffic will be snarled, the auditorium (or outdoor stadium) will be packed, the audience will be six miles from the stage, and the speaker will be boring. Consequently, students should be admonished to limit guests to those who truly wish to be there, since the event itself is tedious and time-consuming.

There are many categories of college graduates. Some of the most common include:

- Don't want to be there types
- Ho-hum grads
- Weepy, sad-it's-over seniors
- Excited and exuberant grads

Parents must be prepared to respond appropriately, whatever category their graduate is in. Make sure you find out, in advance, how he or she is reacting to the impending ceremony.

Graduates Who Don't Want to Be There

Some students aren't particularly excited about graduation. A small number of graduates feel the ceremony is an unnecessary burden. This attitude leads to one of two responses.

Many times nontraditional students have jobs that preclude going to graduation. Other nontrads just don't want to sit with a bunch of kids in a hot building or in the hot sun for three hours. A few young students are either so hostile to the institution itself or to the pomp and circumstance of the ritual that they will come up with any excuse to avoid attending. If Mom and Dad don't mind not going, it is possible, in most schools, to petition to get out of attending.

A word of caution about skipping graduation: *It only happens once. If you miss it, you can't go back.*

This reality applies to both parents and graduates. As with a high school senior prom and other milestones, staying away may seem like a great idea at the time, but later a sense of remorse builds. Thoughts of "what if?" or "what was it like?" may enter your mind after some time passes. Therefore, only those who are absolutely certain that missing the show won't bother them should take this route.

A second possibility is that the student doesn't want to go, but Mom and Dad truly wish to be there. This scenario requires a real heart-to-heart talk. Parents may wish to gently suggest how important it is to them, and remind the reluctant youngster how much Mom and Dad contributed to obtaining the degree. If your relationship is even the slightest bit good, the graduating senior should abide by your wishes and go anyway. Point out that it's only one afternoon. Thank them for bending to your desire. Reward him or her with things you know will make the affair more meaningful. Photographs taken on this day may have tremendous value in future years. Your child may eventually be grateful that he or she was "forced" to put in an appearance.

Ho-hum Grads

The don't-want-to-be-there crowd is probably a minimal percentage of the senior class. Another relatively modest number of graduates is found in the ho-hum category. These students take the program in stride, feeling that only a minor celebration is in order. For some, this inclination results from an extended stay in college. Fifth- and sixth-year seniors probably have already watched the bulk of their friends graduate, and so are depressed because no friends are left to attend their ceremony. It's tough for fifth-year students to watch everyone else move on, knowing they still have some major hills to climb before it's their turn. The anticipation and excitement of actually finishing become a little more diminished each year. As a result, a quick walk through the line, a couple of cocktails, and the evening is over for these late finishers. As parents, you should try to make the event as meaningful and pleasing as you can. Finishing college was a great victory, no matter how long it took!

Another set of ho-hum types consists of those who expect to continue their education. An undergraduate degree becomes comparable to a high school diploma—important, but not dramatic. These students believe the next piece of sheepskin (M.A.) or the final document (Ph.D.) is the real target, and this first graduation is just a step along the way.

It is still possible for parents of ho-hum grads to enjoy the day. One good approach is to tie graduation to another activity, such as a family reunion, a picnic, or the start of a family vacation. Let the natural "high" that results from commencement carry over into what comes next. While the day itself may not take on the massive significance it does for other students, it still can be enjoyable.

Weepy, Sad-It's-Over Seniors

Ever watch a bride cry all the way through a wedding? Some college graduates do the same thing. They know all their friends will soon scatter across the country, and every aspect of college life will be lost. No more parties, pep rallies, club meetings, student-union hanging out, road trips, games, or anything else that makes life as a student so memorable. To an emotional few, there is a powerful sense of loss. Graduation signals an event that is not quite depressing, but not exactly joyous either.

Parents of the weepy bunch should try to focus their kids on the future. Keep reminding them of all the good things to come in life. Also, patience is important. It's possible a good "boo-hoo" will help them get past these feelings. Of all the groups, these seniors most need to huddle together with their friends to sob and hug, and hopefully to let go. Let them savor this moment. Such genuine emotions are in many ways priceless, to be recalled later when the humdrum routine of life does indeed take over.

Excited, Exuberant Types

The great majority of college grads fall into the exuberant group. They want to yell, scream, sing, dance, and jump for joy. Hopefully they will also want to share the pleasure with you. Every senior class has a couple of members who create funny little signs to wear on their caps and gowns. (By the way, it should not surprise you by now that the cap and gown is another item you have to either rent or buy.) Meanwhile, other graduates try to sneak in beach balls, canned spray string, noisemakers, and other gadgets to make the time more exciting and the afternoon more festive.

There is nothing quite like the exhilaration of youth. They *should* hoop and holler. Enjoy watching them spill over with excitement. Share what you can. Rejoice that they feel this way. Just don't get all goofy and dorky by joining immoderately in their displays of enthusiasm. It's their day, mostly. You should remain a very interested but somewhat passive bystander.

All four classifications of graduates show up each year in the auditorium. Parents will know which category their child is in long before the day arrives. If you have a choice, vote for exuberance. Be supportive no matter how they feel about finishing up.

Parental Reactions to Graduation Day

Parental reactions are similar to those of their youngsters. There is no singular or universal response. Commencement exercises are, in many ways, comparable to Parents Day. That is, parents may be divided into several groups, including:

- Those who don't want to be there
- Those who are ambivalent about being there
- Those who are thrilled to be there.

Find your category, and follow along. For each, there may be some techniques to make the experience better.

Parents Who Don't Want to Be There

It's common for some folks to have the same reaction to graduation as their reluctant kids. If you find yourself dreading even the possibility of a graduation ceremony, be reminded of two factors. First, if your son or daughter attended a church college, you would probably have to go to *two* ceremonies. In the morning, there is something called *baccalaureate*. This boils down to a worship service where everybody thanks God the year is over and the kid made it through, which somehow seems highly appropriate. Then, in the afternoon, you are forced to sit through *commencement,* where the actual degree is conferred. Parents whose children didn't go to a church college owe a debt of spiritual gratitude, since they only have to endure one two-to-three-hour ordeal.

Second, those who don't want to be there should be reminded that graduations are quite similar to weddings and funerals. In all cases, the ritual itself isn't really for the honored guest (wedding couple, dead person, graduate), it's for everybody else. Newlyweds are no nervous they're not going to remember much of anything. That's why so many make videotapes, so they can watch the replay. As far as anyone knows, dead people don't actually hear what is said during their rites, either. So it is with graduates. When the time finally comes and they cross the stage to shake the president's hand and receive the diploma, it goes by so quickly they can hardly recall making the trip.

Consequently, parents who don't want to be there should become aware of all of the purposes of graduation. One goal, in a twisted sense, is to use this forum as a way of saying "thank you" to the people who supported the students. You are invited to this special time of passage and are being honored just as much as the individual wearing the somber and serious outfit. This goes for spouses, grandparents, moms and dads, sons and daughters, and even friends.

To make the time pass better, take lots of photos or video and busy yourself with the details. Be the person in charge of restaurant reservations (and pick the place where *you* want to eat). During the boring parts, ponder the accomplishments of this fine young new alum. Use the time to consider what has become of the little two-year-old who used to sit on your lap and love you to death. In other words, do your own attitude adjustment. Forget the annoying stuff, and concentrate on the good things. Imagine the boring graduation speaker naked! Most of all, recognize how your disdain for this event might affect your youngster. You don't want to spoil his or her day. Be a good sport, and take one for the team.

Those Who Are Ambivalent

Many parents go to countless events they aren't really very excited about attending. At the same time, they know there is some reason why they're supposed to be there. So it is with the ambivalent parent. These folks realize their kids are thrilled to have them around. At the same time, such parents are more than willing to step out of the way and let their child celebrate with friends, which is, after all, what they really want to do. This makes Mom and Dad's part of the day shorter.

To make the most of graduation day, ambivalent parents probably should follow most of the same advice given to those who don't want to attend. Recognize the ways to make your part of the day fun. Enjoy the photo sessions, have a great meal, meet their friends, and sample all of the celebration that you can.

One great technique for ambivalent parents is to couple the graduation ceremony with some kind of grown-up jubilee afterward. Throw your own party and cheer your own personal triumph. Recognize what graduation means:

- freedom from tuition bills
- freedom from requests for book money
- the possibility your child will actually get a job and start earning his or her own keep
- the beginning of a new era, one in which your child can be treated more as a full-fledged adult

Now if these aren't reasons for a wingding of a party, nothing is! Invite your friends over. Pop some champagne. Just don't bore your guests with too much graduation video.

If you don't feel like throwing a grown-up gala, consider other forms of observance. For example, since the great majority of graduation ceremonies occur on the weekend, it's possible for you to take a quick trip to some favorite old haunt and enjoy the bulk of the evening alone. It's a good time to remind yourselves that you'll be living this way most of the time from now on—unless, of course, you've got to go through the whole college rigmarole with another kid or two.

In general, parents who have mixed feelings about the actual commencement program should add something to make the day satisfying or amusing for themselves. Any form of self-reward is certainly in order.

Those Who Are Thrilled to Be There

This category probably holds the bulk of graduate moms and dads. The trick here is to rejoice without being overwhelming and embarrassing to the student. Handled properly, the graduation victory can be enjoyed equally by everyone.

Some people will be attending their very first college commencement exercise when the firstborn finally completes the degree requirements. They arrive wondering what exactly to expect, but brimming with excitement at the same time. The program itself may be disappointing, but not enough to ruin everything else.

For those of you who wish to revel in the entire day, here are a few things to consider:

1. If your son or daughter will be celebrating at home afterward, be the host of the party. Throw the barbecue, and then turn over the basement or outdoors to the kids. Expect to get very little sleep that night.

2. Give your youngster a special graduation present. "Special" does not have to be expensive. A cherished photograph, painting, wall hanging, or book may help your child always remember how much this day means. Something with your signature and a date is nice, since it may become a valuable keepsake.

3. Set up two celebrations. The first should be for family, with everyone invited who want to be there. A good time for this party is the night *before* graduation. Cake, punch, and snacks might be served. The second is for the graduate and his or her friends. In this manner you are able to accommodate the various partying styles of all concerned.

4. Buy lots of film and make sure your camera batteries are charged. Also, before the commencement exercise, check with the

college. Many universities now videotape the entire event and provide students with copies for a modest fee. Other schools hire a professional photographer to take individual photos of each graduate as he or she is handed the diploma. These make great mementos as well.

Some people tend to center their lives on special days (wedding anniversary, favorite holidays, etc.). Therefore, graduation day is met with great anticipation, and these individuals expect it to be an important time. Other people find that their most memorable days just sort of happen. A little preparation can mean both types of families can end up with a day they will fondly remember for a long time.

What Is Everyone Thinking?

A graduation program is similar to a long drive in the car. You're stuck, it's boring, and all you can do is either look at the scenery or daydream. All that idle time needs to be filled somehow. What do kids think about during this time? Here is a glimpse of what your kid may be thinking about during the ceremony.

- I can't wait for the party to start.
- I wish I wasn't already hung over from last night.
- Where am I gonna live this summer?
- I wonder if that company is going to call back and offer me a job.
- Should I propose, or break it off?
- Which side does the tassel go on?
- I can't see Mom and Dad. Oh, well, they're out there somewhere.
- Is this guy ever going to shut up, so we can get this over with?
- I sure hope I passed that last class. Otherwise, I won't actually get a diploma.

So, their minds wander during the ceremony until that one brief moment when they proceed to the front, shake hands, and get the degree. Some are shy, some a little weepy, some stunned, and others are exhilarated. A few showoffs try to make a big demonstrative display out of their little moment in the sun. All too quickly, however, it's back to the chair, and everyone must wait impatiently for the rest of the group to get theirs.

Parents may find a myriad of thoughts passing through their

minds during all of this idle time. Those who have been especially close to their kids throughout the previous twenty years may feel a combination of joy at the accomplishment and loss of their child and their youth.

Other folks focus on worries about job prospects and other elements of the future. Should their son or daughter go to graduate school? If yes, what is Mom and Dad's role at this stage in their educational journey? These and other tough issues furrow the brows of anxious parents.

There will also be a couple of more minor questions. For instance, What do all these *cum laude* things mean, and why doesn't my kid get one? Why are the professors wearing different-colored outfits?

Cum laude means "with honors." *Magna cum laude* signifies higher honors. *Summa cum laude* means your kid is one of those annoying (to other students) dedicated, motivated undergraduates who got practically all A's throughout college, setting a higher grade-curve for other collegians. These egg-heads are the ones who keep standards high at a school. Be proud of any of the three designations. At the same time, it's interesting that most parents find some way to "compete" with other parents during graduation, feeling that their kid deserved higher honors or other awards of one sort or another. There's always a little envy in a graduation hall.

The colors on the various caps and gowns worn by faculty members indicate what kind of degree they hold (education, science, business, and so on). The size of the cowl draped around each neck is based on whether the faculty member holds a master's degree or a doctorate. Usually, the graduation program spells out this information in small print. Take some time to inspect the various forms of headgear they exhibit. It will amuse you and help pass the time.

In the end, whatever emotion or reaction to the graduation ceremony you have, it's important to convey your delight with your child's success. Don't feel guilty if you don't experience the emotions you thought you'd have, or even if you find your mind wandering during the ceremony. Even the most elated parents may eventually find themselves bored, and eager to get all these people through the line and across the stage!

While waiting for everyone else's kid to have his or her thirty seconds of excitement, it's a good idea to ponder the many accomplishments of your graduating senior. Table 16.2 provides a list of some things it takes to make it to this day. Consider these statistics about the typical college career carefully.

TABLE 16.2
College Graduate Statistics
(over a four-year period)

courses taken	40 to 50
classes skipped deliberately	50 to 100
classes arrived at late	another 50 to 100
classes slept through	additional 50 to 100
smart-alec comments made *by* faculty members	dozens
smart-alec comments made *about* faculty members	hundreds
times heart is broken	6 to 12
times broken hearts caused	6 to 12
fights with boyfriend/girlfriend	hundreds
times Grandma/Grandpa died (as an excuse for a late term paper)	20 to 40
aunt/uncle heart attacks (used to miss scheduled tests)	15 to 30
times car trouble kept the student from getting to class (even those who live on campus)	10 to 40
times computer mess-up caused an assignment to be late	30 to 50
letters received from home	50 to 100
letters written to home	5 to 10
requests for money by mail	5–10 (see above)
requests for money by phone	50 to 100
requests for money on signs for television cameras at football games	3 to 6
requests for money in person	20 to 40

CDs purchased	15 to 30
breakfasts purchased after 1:00 P.M.	100 to 150
breakfasts eaten on campus 6:00 A.M.–8:00 A.M.	4
overnighters spent studying	10 to 20
overnighters spent writing term papers	15 to 30
overnighters doing something else	50+
nights spent in jail	0 (you hope!)
football games attended	10 to 15
basketball games attended	10 to 30
rock concerts attended	5 to 15
movies seen	30 to 75
poetry readings, plays, recitals, and classical concerts attended (combined score)	3
road trips taken to meet new heartthrobs in other city	10 to 15
new hairstyles created to attract new guys/gals	3 to 10
new fashion trends followed	4 to 7
complaints about lack of interesting people of the opposite sex on campus	hundreds
Parents Day ordeals	2 to 4
visits home, freshman year	5 to 15
visits home, senior year	2
unbelievable stacks of laundry brought home	5 to 15 (freshmen) 2 (seniors)
times they say to Mom and Dad, "You just don't understand"	300 to 500
times they remember to say "thank you"	3 to 5
new, real, lifelong friends made	3 to 5
lifelong attachments to faculty members made	3 to 5
amount of money given to alumni fundraisers, first five years after graduation	$25.00

Mercifully, all commencement exercises do end. One of the weird experiences most parents encounter occurs in the first few moments following the dismissal from the program. First, almost everyone races for the bathroom, leaving the one with the strongest bladder behind to find the graduate. This becomes a period of feeling dazed and uncertain about how to react. It's over! Expect to endure an interval where you just feel a little off kilter, until things get a little more organized and coherent. If you smoke, you will probably be thrilled that you can now light up.

It's natural for this odd sensation to occur. Next time you're a casual observer at a graduation, watch all the men standing around with their hands in their pockets, wondering what to do. Watch the women fiddle with purses, cameras, and everything else while waiting for everyone to gather together. There is almost a forlorn look that everyone will wear for just a few minutes.

Soon graduates are reunited with parents and friends. Hugs and handshakes become the order of the day. Everyone is still milling around, wondering exactly what comes next. Most want photos of the graduate with their friends, significant others, and maybe a professor or two. Some use the graduation facility as a backdrop for photos. Finally the family will have the good sense to leave, becoming entangled in a massive traffic jam getting out of the parking lot.

From there, meals at overcrowded restaurant, parties, and all other forms of post-event activities begin. Mom and Dad must recognize their place, knowing when to leave and how to politely step aside so their kids can carouse and rejoice.

On the drive home, you probably will feel old. Well, maybe you *are* old, so don't make a big deal about it! But don't think this means you're done with parenting this particular young person. Some coaching and counseling remains. Here is a list of the coming attractions:

- how to find a job
- how to plan a wedding
- how to choose a graduate school
- where to live in the meantime
- how to pay your own bills and stop asking for money
- what it means to go to work rather than to class

Many meaningful and important conversations remain. You'll

probably find these talks about jobs and weddings are easier, since you've had these experiences. If your child is considering graduate school, and you've never gone yourself, there may be some investigating to do before you render any advice.

The Cool of the Evening

Finally, after all the talks about what comes next are over, when all the hoopla and merriment of graduation day has subsided, and when your child is placed in his or her next living arrangement, take some time to sit quietly on your front porch or in your favorite outdoor spot. Do this when the sun is about to set, the winds have died down for the day, and the warmth of spring still lingers. It's the cool of the evening. The days and weeks that follow graduation day are like the cool of the evening in the parenting process. Enjoy this time of the day as well as this time in your life. Ponder where you are and where you have been. You have survived.

Kids don't really notice the cool of the evening. They are so busy and active that they forget to take the time to absorb the small wins and happy times. As a parent, it's helpful to recall the semesters when your son or daughter made the dean's list (the good one, based on all A's and B's in a given term). Remember the excited phone calls when he told you he made the team, or was promoted to first string. Recollect how she proudly announced she was president of a major on-campus club and was going to lead them to new heights! Ponder the possibilities the future now brings. Statistics indicate that the odds are improved that they will earn more money, marry successfully, enjoy more varied experiences of travel and culture. Good things can be expected for your new college graduate.

The transformation from freshman to senior college student has been amazing to watch. It was probably fun, stirring, tedious, and traumatic all at the same time. Parents may find that they have changed along the way as well. You probably have let go of some of the frustration of raising a teenager. You may be a little intimidated by the fact that you are now dealing with an adult.

No matter how you respond to the completion of college, always remember: *You played a big part in this conquest of college!* You're entitled to feel proud not only of the new graduate, but also of yourself. Commencement, as nearly every graduation speaker will remind you, means "beginning." It's time to move on. Still, before you do, savor the moment. Never forget to celebrate the victories and shared moments of joy, no matter how great or small. They are the things that make parenting one of the most enriching and inspiring parts of life.

You, as a parent, have done much more than survive. Your child, in all his or her glory, is a college graduate. Congratulations, in advance, for the day when you (and they) reach this goal!

INDEX